# THE LETTERS OF SISTER VA

**Sister Vajirā** (Hannelore Wolf, 14 October 1928 – 7 December 1991)
Photo: Harris Photographers, Colombo, 57 Galle Road;
Summer 1955, as a nun after the ordination.

ÑĀṆAVĪRA THERA

# THE LETTERS OF SISTER VAJIRĀ

(1961-1962)

Path Press Publications

First edition: January 2010
ISBN 978 94 6090 002 0

Path Press Publications
*www.pathpresspublications.com*

## EDITOR'S FOREWORD

THIS BOOK PRESENTS the life and practice of a female renunciate who had to go through much mental turbulence and anxiety on her quest for the path. Her name was Hannelore Wolf. She was born on 14th October 1928 in Hamburg, Germany. In 1955 Hanna went to Ceylon (nowadays Sri Lanka) and with a new name, Vajirā, entered a nuns' community (*dasa-sīl-upāsikā*) near Colombo. Despite the difficulties of her life, she took the Buddha's Teaching to heart, and with much enthusiasm sought to experience the Dhamma for herself. Soon after she arrived in Ceylon she became skilled in languages (English and Pāli), and studied the Suttas (the Buddha's Discourses), as well as existentialist (phenomenological) philosophy. After corresponding with Ven. Ñāṇavīra Thera and contemplating his instructions she attained a fundamental and liberating understanding of the Dhamma: according to Ven. Ñāṇavīra, she attained stream entry: *sotāpatti*. This experience had such a powerful impact on her, that she suffered some kind of 'breakdown' and was unable to function normally in society. Shortly after this experience she disrobed, was repatriated to Germany and for the rest of her life lived on her own without having any close relations with anybody else. She died in December 1991.

Her correspondent, Ven. Ñāṇavīra Thera, was born as Harold Musson in Aldershot, England, in 1920. He was educated at Cambridge, where he read mathematics and modern languages. Together with his friend Osbert Moore (later Ven. Ñāṇamoli) he left England in 1948. Both were ordained as novices at the Island Hermitage in 1949, and a year later both received bhikkhu ordination in Colombo. After training at the Island Hermitage, Ven. Ñāṇavīra Thera moved to Bundala, a more secluded area in the south-east of the island, where he lived as a hermit in a *kuṭi* (hut). There he composed his magnum opus: *Notes on Dhamma*. He died in 1965 by his own hand. His collected writings can be found in two books: *Clearing the Path* and the forthcoming *Seeking the Path*.

It is most fortunate that Sister Vajirā's letters are now available. They are being published here for the first time. Much of this material was at one time thought to have been lost. At some point in 1968 or early 1969, while the American monk Ven. Bodhesako (at that time known as Bhikkhu Ñāṇasuci) resided at the Island Hermitage, he was shown a manila envelope that was kept there. A note in Ven. Ñāṇavīra Thera's handwriting stated that the envelope contained Sister Vajirā's letters to him and that they should be shown only to bhikkhus who were known to be discreet. Eventually, Ven. Bodhesako made a copy of these letters by hand, adding, in a coloured ink, all the marks and comments Ven. Ñāṇavīra made on the originals. The originals were latter mailed to Ven. Ñāṇasumana, an American disciple of Ven. Ñāṇavīra who lived in his *kuṭi* in Bundala. After the death of Ven. Ñāṇasumana in 1970 all these papers were lost and never recovered. Only the copies survived, which also appeared and disappeared over the years, until they were eventually transcribed as a type-written manuscript. This manuscript was kept by the English monk Ven. Ariyesako (who was a member of Ven. Bodhesako's Path Press team), who eventually gave it to Stephen Batchelor for safekeeping. Stephen subsequently returned the manuscript to Path Press.

Path Press has now decided to publish the reconstructed correspondence between Sister Vajirā and Ven. Ñāṇavīra as a separate book. Since Ven. Ñāṇavīra had a strong objection to the publication of the letters before the death of Hanna, we wanted to make sure that we were doing the appropriate thing even though we knew that Hanna had passed away in 1991. Fortunately, we found Ven. Bodhesako's letter to Hanna with the request for permission to publish parts of her letters to Ven. Ñāṇavīra in *Clearing the Path*. He wrote to her: 'With publication of this volume it is our hope that (as you wrote in your letter of 25th January) "Many will have a better chance" to understand Dhamma.' As a reply she sent via Helmuth Hecker this letter:[a]

München, 8.4.86
Schulstr. 33, 2105 Seevetal 3

Mein lieber Hellmut!

Besten Dank für die Weiterleitung des Briefs aus Ceylon. In derselben Sache, nämlich der Veröffentlichung des Buches "Clearing the Path", möchte ich Dich freundlich bitten, gemäß beiliegendem Brief, dorthin mitzuteilen, daß ich über deren Absichten informiert bin, und daß ich keine Einwände hinsichtlich der Veröffentlichung habe.
Ich nehme an, daß Dir dieses möglich sein wird. Es ist auch etwas eilig. Für eine kurze Mitteilung hinsichtlich dieser Sache wäre ich Dir dankbar.
Meine besonders herzlichen Grüße an Paul Debes, Irmtraut Anders und Familie!
Mit freundlichen Grüßen,
Deine Hanna Wolf

a. Translation: see Editorial Note 75, p. 124.

To make even more sure that we were acting correctly, we discussed the publication of the letters with the bhikkhus involved with Path Press. No one objected that we publish them. Subsequently, Gerolf T'Hooft carefully retyped the letters and prepared them for publication as they appear in this book.

The content of the letters remains unedited. Only minor spelling corrections and layout changes have been made. The reconstructed correspondence also includes all Ven. Ñāṇavīra's known replies to Sister Vajirā's letters, which were already published in *Clearing the Path* (though his last letter was not part of the 1987 edition of the book). Ven. Ñāṇavīra's letters have been edited from rough drafts of letters to Sister Vajirā, the final copies having been burnt by their recipient.

Ven. Ñāṇavīra also showed the letters to some of his closest friends. In August 1964 he sent a package with all Sister Vajirā's letters to the Sri Lankan judge Lionel Samaratunga. In a separate letter (L. 99/106) he describes the background of the correspondence extensively. Because this letter is such a good starting point we inserted it here as the 'Introduction'. As an 'Afterword' we include the remaining letters of Ven. Ñāṇavīra to Mr Samaratunga concerning Sister Vajirā, which serve as a commentary to the events described.

For Hanna's 'Biography' we would like to express our gratitude to Dr. Helmuth Hecker and Raimund Beyerlein for allowing us to publish it here. It originally appeared in: *Lebensbilder deutscher Buddhisten, Ein bio-bibliographisches Handbuch, Band II: Die Nachfolger*, Konstanz, 1997, chapter 119, p. 374-386. We are grateful to Ven. Mettiko for providing a translation from German.

'A Note on Phassa' (part of *Notes on Dhamma*) is often referred to in the letters between Ven. Ñāṇavīra and Sister Vajirā but not quoted by them. For those who do not have access to *Notes on Dhamma* [Path Press Publications, 2009], we have provided this note at the end of the book (with translations of the Pali texts by Ven. Ñāṇavīra) as an 'Appendix'. (An online version of *Notes on Dhamma* is available at *www.nanavira.org*).

We have also added some 'Editorial Notes' with comments and translations of Pāli texts (translated by Ven. Ñāṇavīra in *Notes on Dhamma*, and the editors with the support of Ven. Chandako and others). The 'Glossary' of Pāli words which appears here is based on Ven. Ñāṇavīra's *Notes on Dhamma*, and Ven. Ñāṇamoli's *A Pali-English Glossary of Buddhist Technical Terms* [BPS, 1994].

* * *

This book is presented to the reader as an invitation to reflect on certain ideas about the Buddha's Dhamma without rejecting or blindly accepting anything written in its pages. We hope that reading and contemplating these texts will have beneficial results.

B.H.

## ABBREVIATIONS

| | |
|---|---|
| A. | Aṅguttara Nikāya |
| *CtP* | *Clearing the Path, Writings of Ñāṇavīra Thera (1960-1965)*, [Path Press, 1987], Path Press Publications, 2010 |
| D. | Dīgha Nikāya |
| Dhp. | Dhammapada |
| L. # | Letter by Ñāṇavīra Thera (*CtP*-numbering 1987/2010) |
| M. | Majjhima Nikāya |
| Miln. | Milindapañho |
| *NoD* | *Notes on Dhamma*, Path Press Publications, 2009 |
| *NP* | A Note on Paṭiccasamuppāda (first part of *NoD*) |
| S. | Saṃyutta Nikāya |
| Sn. | Suttanipāta |
| *SN* | Shorter Notes (third part of *NoD*); words written in smallcaps [e.g. ATTĀ, ANICCA, CETANĀ, PHASSA] refer to the sub-entries of 'Shorter Notes' |
| *StP* | *Seeking the Path, Early Writings of Ñāṇavīra Thera (1954-1960)*, Path Press Publications, 2010 |
| SV. # | Letter by (or concerning) Sister Vajirā |
| Ud. | Udāna |
| Thīg. | Therīgāthā |

# CONTENTS

*

Everything printed in red is, in the original manuscript, in Ven. Ñāṇavīra Thera's handwriting. This includes marginal comments and sidelining (indicating significance) and both wavy lines and 'X' (indicating disagreement or querry). Footnotes indicated by *letter* (**a**, **b**, **c**…) are Sister Vajirā's or Ven. Ñāṇavīra Thera's and are placed at the bottom of the page; those indicated by *number* (**1**, **2**, **3**…) are editorial notes and can be found at the end of the book.

# INTRODUCTION

**[L. 99/106] 15 August 1964**

Dear Mr. Samaratunga,

I am sending you, under separate (registered) cover, a package of Sister Vajirā's letters to me, written between the beginning of November 1961 and the end of January 1962. I think you will find them of interest, but for obvious reasons they should be treated as confidential. Without, for the present, commenting on the letters themselves, I shall fill in the background for you.

Up to 1961 I do not recall having met Sister Vajirā on more than one occasion, and then for hardly more than a minute. Before then, in 1956, I think, I wrote an article, 'Sketch for a Proof of Rebirth'[1], which was printed in the *Buddha Jayanti*. Sister Vajirā read the article and wrote to me saying that she was much impressed by it, and asking whether she could translate it. I gave my consent, but owing (partly) to a misunderstanding I was not satisfied with her translation and it was never published. We exchanged a few slightly acrimonious letters (neither of us being inclined to mince our words), and the matter was closed. After that, she sent me once or twice some articles she had written, asking me to comment on them. Being busy with my own affairs, I discouraged her from this habit and generally froze her off.

About July 1961 Sister Vajirā wrote to ask whether she could visit me to discuss Dhamma. I agreed, and she came one afternoon for about two hours. Thereafter we had a brief exchange of letters on vegetarianism (which she practised) and also to discuss an English translation of the Dhammapada that she was making. (I have not kept those letters.) Then I sent her my typescript of the NOTE ON PAṬICCASAMUPPĀDA and PARAMATTHA SACCA[2], which I had just finished writing. Sister Vajirā replied with a letter dated 12 November 1961, which is the first of the set I am sending you. She came again to the Hermitage on the

18th November and spent the whole day discussing Dhamma. I did not see her again after that.

At the beginning of the correspondence I did not expect anything very much to come of it but, having the time to spare, I was prepared to go on with it until it seemed pointless to continue. As it progressed, however, I found that she was giving attention to what I was saying, and I decided to keep it alive even though she seemed inclined to let it die. Towards the end (after her letter of 6 January 1962) I began to think it is possible that something might happen, without however really expecting that it would. Anyway, I wrote my letter of the 10th January (of which you will find a rough draft[3]) with the thought, 'If this doesn't do it, nothing will'. Even so, her letter of the 21st came as a surprise, and I was delighted. (This letter alone was enough to convince me, and the next one, of the 23rd, came only as confirmation, though it was nonetheless welcome for all that!)

Things were now happening much too fast for me to keep up with them. (It seemed—and seems—to me that she went through in about five days what took me three months and a half—though of course our circumstances were different—and I was quite unprepared for her subsequent behaviour, though she gave me notice of it at the end of the letter of the 23rd.) Evidently what happened was that with the sudden release of the central tension all her compensating tensions found themselves out of work and began aimlessly expending themselves this way and that, and some time was required before she found a new position of stable equilibrium. I asked the Ven. Thera for a report, and he replied (as I *hoped* he would) that although she had recovered she 'seemed to be a changed person'.

I was not at all pleased when she was bundled out of the country before I was able, as the doctors say, to 'follow up the case'. But later reports seem to confirm that she has remained 'a changed person'. The fact that she now seems to have lost interest in the Dhamma and no longer associates with her former Buddhist friends is a good sign, not a bad one—when one has got what one wants, one stops making a fuss about it and sits down quietly. (In my own case, I had previously been maintaining a continuous correspondence with the Ven. Ñāṇamoli Thera about the Dhamma, and then afterwards I stopped it entirely, finding it pointless. There was no longer anything for me to discuss with him, since the former relationship of parity between us regarding the Dhamma had suddenly come to an end. I could only have renewed the correspondence if he had been made aware—which he was not—of our new relationship.) Anyway, even though I have only Sister Vajirā's letters to go on, I do not see any reason to doubt her statement (23 January 1962) that she has ceased to be a *puthujjana*. Perhaps I should add that though she seems to have had a fairly strong emotional attitude towards me (as 'representing the arahat'), this has not been mutual. At no time have I found myself emotionally interested in her in any way, though, naturally enough, from the point of view of Dhamma I regard her with a friendly eye.

LETTERS FROM SISTER VAJIRĀ (UPĀSIKĀ HANNAH WOLF) AT HEENATIGALA, TALPE, GALLE, TO ÑĀṆAVĪRA THERA AT THE ISLAND HERMITAGE, DODANDUWA, AND BUNDALA, HAMBANTOTA. 12 NOVEMBER 1961 TO 25 JANUARY 1962.

*

*These letters are strictly confidential* and must on no account be made public before the death of Sister Vajirā. They should not be removed from the Island Hermitage under any condition, and should be shown only to bhikkhus who are known to be discreet.

Ñāṇavīra
27 July 1962

**[SV. 1]** **12 November 1961**

Dear Venerable Ñāṇavīra,

I am happy enough to have received from you many kind and instructive lines (also your letter dated 9. inst., thank you), whilst I, on the other hand, have not been able to bring about *one* letter to you. I am sorry for it. I have an excitable time, as it happens off and on. Anyway, I hope to make up for it *when I come on the 18. inst.* (or will I make it worse?). After you have so kindly provided a basis for discussion even (by sending your *Paṭiccasamupāda* essay [4] to me, which could have been written for me), it would be a shame to me not to seize this opportunity. I will be coming straight by car; if it is not unsuitable, early in the morning, starting from here between 6 and 6.30 a.m. Kindly inform the Mahāthera about it, and ask him to have me fetched across the water. I will return in the same way in the evening. Nobody is to accompany me (though many would like), save a small girl who will take my *dāna* with her and attend on me (you might perhaps not find it difficult to get a *dāna* for me, but since these people here like to do it in that way it can be left at that). On that day, I hope to have ample occasion to refer to your essay. By the way, I made two copies of it. These are sent ahead enclosed (because I do not like to encounter your possible displeasure over it, I did not ask your permission, directly), so that you may have time to consider whether you would like to let me have one (the copy of my copy, for there I did not take so much of trouble to correct minor mistakes). The copies of mine were duly compared with the original with the help of two of my friends here who are well-educated girls. I could not type the appendix. I cannot say yet whether or not I still might do it. I would like to of course.

Regarding the letter dated 3. inst. I recognized Mr. Perera for just that type of individual that you describe him. That was also the reason why I destroyed his letter, though I was conscious that the address was on it. It was purely incidentally that I mentioned the whole thing to you, even though I feel that the problem, to Mr. P., and to the degree that he really sees it, *is bound up with you very personally*. I can do nothing in it, since I have no idea of changing *your* mind. Certainly, the Jīvaka Sutta [5] does not *flatly* prohibit it, but you *could* have known that I meant it to that effect, somehow, and it was therefore not just very nice of you to have *flatly contradicted me* by stating the passage with the gloss as if there were no distinction whatsoever. Mrs. P. happened to quote from your letter *literally*, otherwise I would never have believed it. Now of course, I have become suspicious (whether this question, also to you, be an emotional one). One can also become a vegetarian *after* having resolved one's doubts, in contrast (but not by all means by contradiction) to what you said. If I said that I agree on it in every respect I did so, because, at that time I was not yet suspicious. Whatever it may be, as to Mr. P., I gladly forgive you, anything.

Now the question as such (has it come to it!). In the appendix to my Parinibbāna MS I have a note on *sākara-maddava*[6]. I shall get that note for you, so that you may see from it how *I* would look upon the Jīvaka passage in particular, and the whole thing in general. But I can tell from the very outset that I shall not embark on a horizontal discussion of it, i.e. *to me* it can never be a matter of collecting passages from the Suttas in confutation or evidence of either standpoint, as you will understand from that note also, though of course it might be possible. Kindly remember this in due course. I purposely delay sending the note, though I could write it down by heart (a botheration), because you are very unlikely to appreciate it (in fact, who will? it will never appear in print!); for, after all, how can we hope to agree in theory, if we do not in practice? There may be such people who can bring that about, but not you, anyhow, and I also not, even though, strangely enough, I first thought so.

Now I want to say something regarding your essay, in combination with your previous letter, that cannot be easily expressed by word of mouth (in the presence of others). I do by no means fully grasp every idea of yours found in the manuscript, and, also, I would perhaps not agree with everything that I do grasp, yet I may say in all modesty: *Muhuttam api ce viññū paṇḍitaṃ payirupāsati...*[7] *This is the voice that need be heard*, for *parato ca ghoso yoniso ca manasikāro paccayā sammādiṭṭhiyā upādāya*,[8] no matter whether it be (but) *yatthā-sutaṃ yatthā-pariyattaṃ* (and it can indeed not be other than that). You yourself splendidly deny (and [or] affirm) your fine, and beautifully expressed, ideas (of your previous letter), that is to say, knowing well that my interpretation of the Dhamma has no bearing on it as such, *I must make it known* (i.e. I must interpret it = *yatthā sutaṃ...*). I personally know from what I have experienced some twelve years ago that until I hear that (particular) voice (that appeals to me), I can do nothing but 'watch and pray' (though of course that is much!)—ripeness is all.[9] In other words, every interpretation is strictly individual, but the point from which I gain access to the Dhamma, i.e. where I begin to see for myself, is just so. The Dhamma does not exist apart from being interpreted, for myself and for others, including the Bodhisatta (I use the term in the strict Sutta-usage) as the highest possibility (though of course here not *yathā-sutaṃ*, I mean that interpretation by which he becomes the Buddha).

In this way, I would briefly indicate (there are many more things to be said, but I cannot do more at this moment) and stress, as a vertical section, so to speak, to what you have explained in its horizontal section, that an interpretation, nevertheless, is of fundamental importance. You will understand *what* interpretation, and *of whom to whom*.

One more thing in conclusion. What was made known (*ārocita*) is the light (*āloka*) in which I see it for what it is (Dhamma) and in which I see the Buddha, not otherwise, even if he were present physically. Similarly, if *you* let *me* know (*āroceti*), I can see you for what you are in the Dhamma, not otherwise (it is and is not meant personally; in fact, I was fortunate enough to have seen you long ago, in 56 or so ('Proof of Rebirth')). In this way, also the *Ariya Sāvaka* can be seen in the light of interpretation, and, therefore, to me at least, an interpretation is *the world* (*loka*, that which is manifest on account of its being in the light; though I mean it here in that particular way). And this is the only comfort when it becomes overwhelmingly difficult, and a genuine one.

Respectfully,

V.

**N.B. 12 November**

I think I must make up my mind and send to you enclosed the 'silence' referred to in my last letter, after which I rearranged the Dhammapada. (I do not like to part with it; I have no copy; but there will be no time for you to enter into it, if I would bring it.) It is, I think, not difficult for you to get the idea. You may not at once be able to recognize the 16 *upakilesā* under 'pertaining to the intersocial sphere', but the rest should be clear. I had this thing in mind for a long time, long before the idea of the Dhammapada came up. In fact, there is no need for you to see that connection at all. What I would like to know from you is only whether the 'silence' as such is correct or not.

V.

1. *Rāga-dosa-moha* not symmetrical. The angry are not always the lustful.
2. *Delusion*: self-abnegation is or may be *dosa* rather than *amoha*. Intersocial sphere—many of these things are *dosa*.
3. *Moha-Amoha* not symmetrical except negatively.
4. Hate—Forgiveness—care is necessary.
5. Greed (or Lust?)
6. Do—Jealousy is as much *dosa*.
7. 'Life Divine'.
8. *Bodhipakkhiyā dhammā*?
9. 'Intersocial sphere' is accidental not essential.

**[SV. 2]** A postcard after the meeting at Polgasduwa on the 18th

I could not put forward my 'strongest argument' regarding *upādāna* (please don't fail to refute me, however briefly).

Is the *Anāgāmī* liable to *phassa* or not? Is there *phassa* apart from being *sa-āsava sa-upādāna*? This *upādāna* would fall then under *diṭṭhi*. There are two kinds of *diṭṭhi* (M.117), and to have *sammādiṭṭhi* does not mean to have no *diṭṭhi* (*diṭṭhi* is to means to an end, just as *saddhā* (*asaddhā akataññ*, the *Arahat*)).

I could not proceed to my *āvasa* last night. I am going now.

Respectfully,

V.

**[SV. 3]** **20 November 1961**

Dear venerable Ñāṇavīra,

Before I met you last I had but a very faint idea that your essay was something more than a few loosely connected notes on a vast subject, which partly seemed to need specification also. But now *I know definitely* that this is far from being so. I am about to learn from you the lesson of the 'pedagogical device'—that I have to learn, now or never. And, at the same time, I found the key to perhaps understanding a great deal more of it, or even all. You have indeed succeeded in showing the whole by confining yourself to a few essential particulars. *Abhikkantaṃ, Bhante, abhikkantaṃ, Bhante, ...*

But you have given me indefinitely much more than this, though nothing *apart* from it. This, however, I can neither tell explicitly or impersonally, and, therefore, I shall keep silent. My relations to you ended where they began; there is nothing to be said hereafter. Simply by being what you are, you have rendered me completely *pasanna citta*, as I have never been before, and so brought to a close the crisis I was in. I know that I will be able to stand on a new basis hereafter.

Your essays will be sent to you by registered mail, after I have finished with them (it will take some time). I am not likely to send that note on *sūkara-maddava*. What is the use of it?

Respectfully, and with best wishes,

V.

**N.B. 21 November**

Just now, when I was taking my morning meal, I was able fully to grasp what you have explained under '*omnis determinatio est negatio*'. I knew already yesterday that I would.

The difficulty *cetanā/saṅkhata* has completely dissolved; even though I am inclined to consider that passage (S.III,60) as not original; if it were, it ought to have occurred in the Mahānidāna Sutta.

The obstacle to understanding you was a *verbal* one, just as in the case of *reflexion*, which I did not know to mean mindfulness. After coming to know that significance, purpose, behaviour (intention is clear now), to you, are *nāma*, I have no difficulties.

I personally associate with these first two terms *atthasaṃhita*; in the functioning of *nāma-rūpa-viññāṇa* (& *phassa*), to me, there is no purpose, in other words, there is no purpose in existence; to end it, however, is *atthasaṃhita* (significant).

Further, it is perhaps worthwhile noting that appearance (*rūpa*, here I agree) is manifest in such a way as to entail *nāma as adhivacana*, a naming or, as I would say, evaluating. Significance puts appearance too much away from me, i.e. so as if it existed by itself.

I am in a bit of a hurry, but you will perhaps see the point; it is of no great significance.

[L. 146/156] **21 November 1961**

Dear Upāsikā,[10]

Your argument as I understand it assumes that the *anāgāmī* is liable to *phassa*, and concludes that, since all *phassa* is *sa-āsava sa-upādāna* therefore the *anāgāmī* has *upādāna*. I shall do my best to do as you ask and refute you.

1. I shall take your second question first. 'Is there *phassa* apart from being *sa-āsava sa-upādāna*?' The answer is: no, there is not.

2. 'Is the *anāgāmī* liable to *phassa* or not?' It is evident that your argument depends upon an affirmative answer to this question, and that this, in turn, depends upon the absurdities of a negative answer—i.e. that the *anāgāmī* is *not* liable to *phassa*, which can be truly said only of the *arahat*. It follows from this that your argument is dependent upon the assumption that the question is one that can be answered categorically—if the answer 'no' is absurd, then the answer 'yes' must be correct.

In the Aṅguttara (III, 67/ i,197; IV,42/ ii,46) the Buddha speaks of four kinds of questions: those that can be answered categorically, those that require a discriminating answer, those that require a counter question, and those that must be put aside. Perhaps the question, 'Is the *anāgāmī* liable to *phassa* or not?' cannot be answered categorically and is one that must be set aside.

We know that the *puthujjana* is liable to *phassa*, and that the *arahat* is not. But your question asks about the *anāgāmī*, who is neither *puthujjana* nor *arahat*. It is quite true that if I deny that the *anāgāmī* is liable to *phassa* I confound him with the *arahat*; but it is no less true that if I allow that he is liable to *phassa* I fail to distinguish him from the *puthujjana*. Thus the question cannot be answered.

To this it can be objected that since both *puthujjana* and *anāgāmī* are liable to re-birth, that since neither of them has reached the goal and become *arahat*, in this respect at least, they are indistinguishable, and consequently that the question can in fact be answered affirmatively. It will be noticed, however, that we are now no longer debating whether or not the *anāgāmī* is liable to *phassa*, but whether or not your question 'Is the *anāgāmī* liable to *phassa*?' is answerable. And whether we decide that it is answerable or not depends upon whether we regard the *paṭiccasamuppāda* formulation as a Universal Law (which will include the *sekha*) or as a pedagogical device (which treats the *sekha* as irrelevant). In this way we establish that your argument does not in any way invalidate my view of *paṭiccasamuppāda*[11]; at most it represents a rival point of view; and we are free to choose between them.

3. Can we go further and show that the 'Universal Law' point of view, with its positive assertion that the *anāgāmī* has *upādāna*, may be at variance with the Suttas? Consider this passage: *Evam eva kho...pahīyetha; api ca te evam assa, Dīgharattaṃ vata bho ahaṃ iminā cittena nikato vañcito paladdho; ahaṃ hi rūpaṃ yeva upādiyamāno upādiyim*...[12] We know (M. 44/i,299) that *yo pañcas'upādānakkhandhesu chandarāgo*[13] is *upādāna*; and *cakkhuppādā* is the arising of the *dhammacakkhu* of the *sotāpanna*: *yaṃ kiñci samudayadhammaṃ sabbaṃ tam nirodhadhammanti*.[14] If, then, we adopt the 'Universal Law' point of view and press the question 'Does the *anāgāmī* have *upādāna*?' we meet with the answer that *upādāna* (including, presumably, *kām'upādāna*) is put aside even by the *sotāpanna*; and from this we arrive at the inconvenient conclusion that the *sotāpanna* is an *arahat*. If, on the other hand, we adopt the 'pedagogical device' point of view, we regard the question 'Does the *sotāpanna*, does the *anāgāmī*, have *upādāna*?' as *ṭhapaniya*, and we refrain from asking it; and in this way these difficulties do not arise. When a *puthujjana* obtains the *dhammacakkhu* he there and then ceases to be a *puthujjana* and (in due course) becomes *arahat*.

4. Is *sammādiṭṭhi* to be reckoned as *diṭṭhupādāna*? If the foregoing discussion is accepted this question will not arise; for we are no longer called upon to decide whether or not the *diṭṭhisampanna* (*sotāpanna*) or *anāgāmī* possesses *upādāna*. If not, the following remarks may be relevant.

Though I do not know of any Sutta where *diṭṭhupādāna* is specified in detail, reference to Majjhima 11/i,66 shows that whereas *samaṇabrāhmaṇā* other than the Buddha may be capable of teaching *pariññā* of the first three *upādāna*, it is only the Buddha who can teach *pariññā* of *attavādupādāna*. But if *diṭṭhupādāna* includes *sammādiṭṭhi* then it is beyond the scope of outside *samaṇabrāhmaṇā* to teach *pariññā* of *diṭṭhupādāna*, since *sammādiṭṭhi* is found only within the Buddha's Teaching. From this one might conclude that *sammādiṭṭhi* is not to be reckoned as *diṭṭhupādāna*.

5. *Saupādisesā*. Majjhima 10/i,63 and other Suttas say *sati vā upādisese anāgāmitā*.[15] This, obviously, refers to the *anāgāmī*. But Itivuttaka

44/38[16] speaks of *saupādisesā nibbānadhātu* and *anupādisesā nibbāna-dhātu*. It is clear enough that *upādisesā* cannot refer to the same thing in these two different contexts; for in the first the *upādisesā* of the *anāgāmī* is what distinguishes him from the *arahat* (i.e. some impurity) and in the second *upādisesā* is what distinguishes the 'living' *arahat* from the 'dead' *arahat*. (N.B. It is, strictly, no less improper to apply the word 'life' to an *arahat* than it is the word 'death'.) It is perhaps tempting to look for some significant connexion between the word *upādisesā* and the word *upādāna*, and to attempt to explain these contexts in terms of *upādāna* (possibly also with reference to the phrases *catunnaṃ mahābhūtanaṃ upādāyo rūpaṃ*[17] and *taṇhupādiṇṇa kāye*[18] of Majjhima 28/i,185); but as the Ven. Ñānamoli Thera pointed out to me the words *saupādisesā* and *anupādisesā* occur in Majjhima 105/ii,257 & 259, where they can hardly mean more than 'with something remaining' and 'without something remaining' or 'with/without residue'. This seems to indicate that we are not entitled to deduce from *sati vā upādisese anāgāmitā* that the *anāgāmī* is *sa-upādāna*—all that it implies is that the *anāgāmī* still has something (i.e. some infection) left that the *arahat* does not.

With best wishes,

Ñāṇavīra

**[L. 147/157]** **undated[19]**

Dear Upāsikā,

I do not say that *rūpa* is appearance, I say, rather, that *rūpa* is what appears. *Rūpa, on its own*, cannot appear (and therefore does not exist): in order to appear (or to exist) *rūpa* requires *nāma*; that is to say, it requires feeling and perception. Similarly, *rūpa*, on its own, is not *significant*; for a thing is significant, has an intention, only when it appears *from a certain point of view*; and without *nāma* (and *viññāṇa*) *rūpa* is without a point of view (or orientation). Thus *cetanā* (intention) is *nāma* (see Majjhima 9/i,53) where *nāma* is defined as *vedanā saññā cetanā phassa manasikāra* (attention = point of view, my present point of view is what I am at present attending to)). Without *nāma* we cannot *speak* of *rūpa*, there is no *adhivacana*. But without *rūpa* there is nothing to speak *of*, there is no *paṭigha*.

Though *purpose* is a form of intention, it is rather a crude and obvious form (though useful as a starting-point)—there is intention of a much more subtle nature (which, however, we need not discuss here). The varieties of intention are infinite.

I agree, of course, that there is no purpose in existence, as such. There is no reason why I or anything else should exist. But *when* something exists it is always (negatively) related to other things, i.e. it is significant.

With best wishes,

Ñāṇavīra

[SV. 4] **3 December 1961**

Dear Bhante,

Your letter[20] came into my hands only this morning. Thank you very much. I did not call for my letters for the past two weeks or so, and only now, when I asked the Postmistress to send it to Colombo altogether, I found that a number of letters had been removed from the office already and kept in one of these homes. So I had them brought, among them, unexpectedly, yours.

I will make a few remarks on it. But you are under no obligation to reply to it, though, of course, I would like it (I will call now for letters).

The points 1, 2, and 3 of your letter are fully grasped and greatly appreciated. On principle, there is nothing to be said against it. The outlook is of dynamic force. Yet, I see no absolute need, not in theory at least, to abandon the rival point of mine: the 'universal law' point of view remains as an intellectual possibility, for you, to be refuted, and, as such, is quite justified.

*Diṭṭhupādāna. Attavāda* falls under *diṭṭhi* (so does *sīlabbatta*). From this angle, *samaṇabrāhmaṇā*, other than the Buddha, do *not* have *pariññā* of *diṭṭhupādāna*. (By the way, there is a Sutta (Majjhima) where they are denied the others also.) Now here, the *diṭṭhisampanna*, i.e. *sekha* of any degree, is not liable to *attavāda* on account of his *sammādiṭṭhi ariyā anāsavā lokuttarā maggaṅgā*[21] (the *dhammacakkhu*, as I see it). *At a time* where this prevails in him, he is not liable to any *diṭṭhi* at all, for the others are purely secondary to *attavāda*. However, since it does *not* prevail in him *always*, according to the stage of his *sekhahood*, *at other times*, he is liable to *diṭṭhi*, i.e. *diṭṭhupādāna*, including even *micchādiṭṭhi*, save certain forms of it. In this way, I still maintain that any *sekha* is *saupādāna* = *saupādisesa* (I see no difference here). Refute please.

*Nāma-rūpa*. You are quite right, I do not *fully* know how you look upon it. I meant to say only this much: to the degree that I was able to hear your voice at all, and to remove the hindrances that are of a verbal nature, I understand you quite clearly. You have added to it a little more now, and, in fact, I already proceeded on my own in understanding you, so as to anticipate what you would have to say on significance. I have given very much thought to *nāma-rūpa-viññāṇa*, but there is hardly scope for communicating these ideas by writing. At this stage, it is enough for me to know, as I do, that we *could* come to an agreement with the necessary care. A help to me would be only to use Pali terms.

*Saupādisesa.* In view of the foregoing, I could refrain from entering into it. This question still is liable violently to agitate me, and I have to be careful at the moment. It was non-existent until I came across *Tathāgato anupādisesāya nibbānadhātuyā parinibbāyati*[22] in the Parinibbāna Sutta, which entailed a discussion with Rev. Nyāṇaponika, who pointed out to me It. 44 and, also, the supposed difference between *pañc'upādānakkhandhā* and *pañcakkhandhā*, of which I was completely unaware until then (June '61). Rev. N., however, has refused to answer a letter of mine, in which I pressed him for further explanation. I came to the Dhamma straight from higher mathematics (when I was twenty) and the only thing that fully captured me was that *it leaves no remainder.* Of course, you smilingly will say that indeed it does not, as I am happy enough to know now, but without in any way abandoning the (wretched) point that I will point out now.

*If* there were such a thing as *dve nibbānadhātuya*, was it not by all means due to have occurred in the Bahudhātuka Sutta (M. 115), or in Dīgha 33? If passages like It. 44, or the one quoted by you from the Saṃyutta (*saṅkhārā = cetanā-kāyā*), also due to have occurred in Dīgha 33, appear in perfect isolation from other Suttas, is it not justified to doubt their originality? (Especially when they stand in direct relation to the *traditionally* accepted view, the value of which should be evident.)

The Parinibbāna Sutta, true enough, has *anupādisesā nibbānadhātu.* To me, however, there is only one *Nibbāna* (*dhātu*), and that is always *anupādisesā.* The *arahat* is *parinibbuta*, and the Suttas make no such absurd distinctions as 'living' and 'dead' *arahat.* There is distinction between a dead person and one having attained to *saññā-vedayita-nirodha*[23], that is all.

It is the typical, as I call it, horizontal way of the Commentators to have invented here a *saupādisesā nibbānadhātu*, which would, as they imagined, nicely correspond to the *anupādisesā nibbānadhātu* of the Parinibbāna Sutta. And why, because, evidently, they had lost all appreciation for such an *absolutely positive* statement, which calls for no speculation. The It. 44 is absolutely unintelligible. If it is abondoned, we are no longer obliged to see in *saupādisesa* anything but (of course) *upādāna.* After all is it not *taṇhākkhaya* that is *khīṇāsava*? In other words, so long as there is *taṇhā*, there is *upādāna.* I do really not see why you should offer so many objections to this! Don't fail to refute me.

I have returned your essays to Bundala by registered mail. I am sure you duly received them. It is hardly possible to express through what stages I passed after the 18., especially since I know now that you eschew anything personal. (Though, of course, I also know that my being personal and your being impersonal are no incompatible extremes, and I would therefore not hesitate to tell you anything, but, having got so far, I can manage the rest also, without doing so.) But you will perhaps allow me to say that I am boundlessly 'indebted' to you; without you, I would not have been able to make such efforts as I did during the last two weeks. It is no exaggeration to say that you have given new life to me. I have cut myself away from the literary work entirely. It was due, but I hadn't the strength as yet. I venture to say that it won't take me long to become refuge to myself now, in the way you said that day. It would be extremely kind of you if you would allow me to have some connection with you by writing, even in my own way, if need be; but it is not necessary, if it be a nuisance to you. Just as you please. I can find you also otherwise. I hope you are in the best of health after your return.

With deepest veneration,

V.

## THE WAY IN ITS ACTUALITY

The Teaching of the Buddha converges in the *Four Noble Truths*: Suffering, its Origin, its Cessation, and the Way to its Cessation (*dukkha-nirodha-gāmini-paṭipadā*). The Way, also called the Middle Way, is the Noble Eightfold Path, in its three sections (*khandhā*), Morality, Concentration, and Wisdom.

By its nature, the Way points to the Goal, which is the utter destruction of suffering. But not only does it *point* to the Goal, it also achieves its accomplishment *in* the Goal, and not otherwise. It is in the *Arahat*, whose cravings are quenched forever, and who is perfectly cooled down, that the Middle Way fully comes to life. To all other men, the Middle Way is the phenomenon to be cultivated (*bhāvetabba dhamma*) *par excellence*. It essentially relates to the *future*—though not at any rate distant—result of absolute imperturbable emancipation (*akuppa-ceto-vimutti*), and, for this, sets aside anything *trespassing* on its principles, step by step. The Middle Way, thus, is dynamic, not static. It comes to be through the best possible approximation to the ideal at each individual instant of application.

Only when thus viewed in its relation to the Goal, the Way reveals its actuality as the *Dukkha-nirodha-gāmini Paṭipadā*[24], the Course-to-end-ill. Implying a complete set of morals, the Way is not a code of morals, but of *spiritual effort*. Attaching every importance to morality, it does not establish itself in morals, but, *by means of intelligence*, in the Goal. For morals, when adhered to (*parāmaṭṭha*[25]) can only lead to a better, but not everlasting, existence, while the Way aims at liberation from all existence.

Thus, The Way, rightly viewed and applied, must be understood as a most intricate co-operation of *all* its links, and more particularly so, of Right Understanding, Right Effort, and Right Mindfulness, in application to each link, as beautifully set forth in the Cattārisaka Sutta: Right Understanding, at the respective moment of application, is the initial impulse (*sammādiṭṭhi pubbaṅgama*[26]) for Right Effort, and Right Mindfulness is the safeguarding survey of the field of one's inner labour. And thus by mental discrimination initiated and sustained effort rightly may be called the application of the Middle Way, for it is bound to culminate in that unique *Sammā Samādhi* connected with immediate Fruition.

Vajirā
Bosat 1960

*incidentally*
need not be returned
*or commented upon*

## [SV. 5] 4 December 1961

Since I do not feel quite fit for meditation today, I would like to take down some of my ideas on *nāma-rūpa*. This will be the first time that I communicate them, at least from the *nāma*-aspect. The scheme on *rūpādānakkhanda*, which I hope to send as well, is known to Dr. Hecker. I wrote down these ideas some years ago in German, but since lost sight of it. I will largely have to depend on what is present to my mind only, for my whole writing equipment etc. has been removed from my *āvāsa*. I can, therefore, not give you very detailed references. But if this should prove an obstacle kindly let me know.

There is no difficulty, I think, in establishing that experience, or *an* experience, is *nāma-rūpa-viññāṇa*. [Experience, in German, is *Erleben* or *Erfahrung*.] Should it be possible to call it *pātubhūta* or, better, *pātubhava*? If now experience is considered the Gordian knot to be untied, *nāma* would be the loose end from which to start. As I unravel it, *rūpa* dissolves completely, being merely a Fata Morgana, and, thereby, experience itself, *leaving no remainder*.

The five factors of *nāma*, one and all, are factors of evaluating (*werten*) *rūpa*. *Nāma-rūpa*, thus, 'that-which-appears-and-its-evaluation'. I would prefer writing (e)value(ation), in order to show the twofold aspect of experience that is implied here, i.e. passively (*kamma-vipāka*), 'what-appears-and-its-value, and, actively (*kamma*), 'what-appears-and-its-evaluation'. [*Kamma* and *kammavipāka* are condition for each other.] This is, in my opinion, what the passage Mahānidāna Sutta, in essence, reveals; *liṅga* etc., in each case (either of *nāma* or *rūpa*) and instant (i.e. from which of the two an experience springs), is *vipāka*.[a]

Now something about the characteristic features of each factor. *Phassa* stands out from the rest. If the others are evaluation of what appears, *phassa* makes possible experience itself. Similarly as a self-acting machine the (experience) functions automatically (*nāma-rūpa*), provided it has contact (with the source from which it draws its energy), *phassa* not only determines experience for *what* it is, but also for *that* it is at

---

a. That is to say, a table appears to me *as a table* not because it *is* a table, but because it has *previously* (not necessarily previous to this life) been diversified (*papañceti*) as such. In other words, *papañca saññāsaṅkhā* is *vipāka*. You are aware of M. 18.

all, *sāsava saupādāna*, that is to say. *Phassa*, as contrasted to the other factors of evaluating *rūpa*, not only has part in, but *is* experience. *Phassa* is, therefore, *erlebensidentisch*, identical with experience.

Dhātu-vibhaṅga sutta, please

There are only two factors more that are of almost equal interest than *phassa*, i.e. *cetanā* and *manasikāra*. On these two, however, you have said already much more than to cover my own ideas. For the present, therefore, I can confine myself to this much.

In the light of your latest remarks on *manasikāra*, I may perhaps assume that *reflexion*, which was a stumbling-block to me earlier, to you, is *manasikāra*, or, probably, *yoniso manasikāra*, even though you associated it that day with mindfulness (*sati*). But that was, I feel, only to make it easier for me to get over my perplexity. At any rate, *reflexion*, in my opinion, would not reach the level of *yoniso manasikāra* as a translation.

I will now try to get that scheme ready and enclose it.

With deepest veneration,

V.

N.B. Regarding the scheme. The red marks indicate uncertainty. You will at once notice that the *jhānas* are missing. Can you place them? You need not return it.

Two things more. Do you share the traditional view that *magga-* and *phala-*attainments are instantaneous? (i.e. that the *phala-* follows the *magga-*attainment instantaneously). And you always stress that memory is not on the same level of certainty than immediate experience, including even the *abhiññas*. I do not agree with it. Remembering e.g. my previous existences can certainly form part of my *aparapaccayañāṇa* of *jāti*.

No. (Okkantika Saṃy.)[27]

V.

**TIVIDHENA RŪPA SAṄGAHO = NAVA SATTĀVĀSĀ**
**(satta viññāṇaṭṭhitiyo + Rūpa No. 11 and Arūpa No. 4)**
**= CATASSO VIÑÑĀṆAṬṬHITIYO**

**SATTA VIÑÑĀṆAṬṬHITIYO (exclude 10-16)**

| Ti-loka | Ti-vidhena Rūpa saṅgaha | | No. | Kāyā | Satta Viññā-naṭṭhi-tiyo | Aṭṭha Vimokha | Aṭṭha Abhibhā-yatanāni |
|---|---|---|---|---|---|---|---|
| KĀMA-LOKA | Sani-dassana-sa-paṭigha rūpa | Tisso Kāmūpapattiyo (Vi-nipātikā, manussa 5 & 6) | | Vinipātikā (apāya) | 1) nānatta-kāyā-nānatta-saññino | 1) rūpī rūpaṁ passati | 1,2) ajjhattaṁ rūpa-saññī eko bahiddhā rūpaṁ passati... |
| | | | | Tiracchānā | | | |
| | | | | Nirayā | | | |
| | | | | Petā | | | |
| | | | | Asurā | | | |
| | | | | Manussā | | | |
| | | | | Devā (26: kama 6, rūpa 16, arūpa 4) | | | |
| | | | 1. | Catummahār. | | | |
| | | | 2. | Tavatiṁsā | | | |
| | | | 3. | Yāmā | | | |
| | | | 4. | Tusitā | | | |
| | | | 5. | Nimmāna-rati | | | |
| | | | 6. | Paranimmita-vasavati | | | |
| | | | | Pajāpati | | | |
| RŪPA-LOKA | | Tisso sukhūpapattiyo (7, 5, 3) | 1. | Brāhmakāyikā | 2) nānatta-kāyā-ekatta-saññino | | |
| | | | 2. | Ābhā | 3) ekatta-kāyā-nānatta-saññ'no | 2) Ajjhattaṁ arūpa-saññī eko bahiddhā rupāni passati (=Aṭṭha Abhibhāyatanā) | 3, 4, 5, 6, 7, 8) ajjhattaṁ arupa-saññī rupāni passati.... |
| | | | 3. | Parittābhā | | | |
| | | | 4. | Appamanābhā | | | |
| | | | 5. | Abhassarā (pītibhakkhā) | | | |
| | | | 6. | Subhā | 4) ekatta-kāyā-ekatta-saññī | | |
| | | | 7. | Parittasubhā | | | |
| | | | 8. | Appamānasubhā | | | |
| | | | 9. | Subhakiṇṇā | | | |
| | | | 10. | Vehapphalā | | | |
| | | | 11. | Abhibhū | | | |
| | | | | Asañña-satta | | | |
| | | Anāgāminu | | PAÑCA SUDDHĀVĀSĀ | | 3) Subhan' t' eva adhimutto hoti | |
| | | | 12. | Avihā | | | |
| | | | 13. | Atappā | | | |
| | | | 14. | Sudassā | | | |
| | | | 15. | Sudassī | | | |
| | | | 16. | Akaniṭṭhā | | | |
| ARŪPA-LOKA | ani-dassana sa-paṭigha rūpa | | 1. | Ākāsānañcāyatana | 7) 6) 5) | 6) 5) 4) | |
| | | | 2. | Viññāṇānañcāyatana | | | |
| | | | 3. | Ākiñcaññāyatana | | | |
| | ani-dassana a-paṭigha rūpa | | 4. | Nevasannānāsannā-yatana | | 7) | |
| | | | | Saññā-vedayita-nirodha | | 8) | |

**[SV. 6]** **13 December 1961**

Dear Bhante,

Your letter dated 7. inst. arrived today. Thank you very much. I also received in between your post card.

That you have replied to me in this fashion is not altogether unexpected, though, naturally, not just 'welcome'; but since you did reply at all, and since you have expressed that you do not 'absolutely discountenance' my writing to you either, I am afraid I have no other way than continuing our correspondence. I do it with a feeling of discomfort, knowing that it evidently disturbs you; but *you are free* to discontinue it; it is in your hands.

I shall try to go through your letter in the same succession that you have chosen.

1, 5, 7. There is no need for me to take up your apparent challenge and consider whether or not I regard myself an *Ariyasāvaka*. Your whole argument, which, as such, is quite in agreement with my own ideas, seems to point to a misunderstanding, to which to have given rise certainly is my own fault. The passages referred to in our talk and correspondence are the *first* and *only* ones that I ever doubted. I have tried to impress on you what this question means to me; but, evidently, I failed utterly in being understood. Instead, I have to share the fate of the mere 'competent mathematician', that I am not! It is *for this question* that I will carry on our discussion, against my feelings of discomfort, until you yourself end it; if not something better should happen. I know now that it is a matter of *getting at it* at all. But I shall find my way, even though you accept only a very few approaches to it, unfortunately. In order, then, that you possibly may cease regarding me a child that has not yet done with intellectual play things, and that must therefore be 'kept occupied', please know that I have a *definite purpose* in writing to you; once it is achieved I shall cease from doing so. Since I did not meet someone like you earlier, *you are the cause*, so to speak, that this question has become acute, and you ought, therefore, not avoid answering it.

It should be amply clear now that my attitude towards our texts is the very opposite of rejecting anything frivolously. My fault was to have expressed my views provokingly, not knowing that you are susceptible here.

Your remark on my supposed 'fondness of tidy charts', even if it was not meant unkindly, is absolutely irrelevant; though, in other ways, I ought perhaps be reminded of Kisāgotamī Therī[28]. I do this for no other purpose than compressing a great amount of ideas, i.e. the very opposite of sterility, into a small compass. Does it mean that, also to this, you will not reply, only because it does not appeal to you?

2. Save the Vinaya, I also accept as authentic the same books; but I do not go so far as to regard any discussion on individual points as entirely out of the way. I have found passages in the Itivuttaka that contradict passages in the Dīgha and Majjhima; these have undermined my confidence in that collection. But here our agreement is of greater importance, for it is the *interpretation* that can matter, even in that particular point of the *dve nibbānadhātuya*. In this way, it is interpreted as being a 'remnant of *previous* clinging'. But this you certainly reject, do you not?

14.12. But, however this may be, should it really escape you that my accepting *certain books* from the Tipiṭaka, and rejecting others, is on exactly the same level than accepting *certain passages*, and rejecting others; I do the first thing in order to restrict passages to be rejected to the minimum, or even to avoid it altogether, and for this alone my doing so is justified. That is to say, if I cease to be on the watch after having made my general choice, I indeed seat comfortably in a self-made cage, imagining that I am free, and am, ultimately, no better off than someone assuming that only Abhidhamma leads to *Nibbāna*.

*Anaññāte aññatamānī*[29] has two aspects: I can either see Dhamma-Vinaya in what is *not* Dhamma-Vinaya, or I can fail to see Dhamma-Vinaya in *what is* Dhamma-Vinaya. In this way, if the passage Itivuttaka is *not* authentic, you would be as much in the wrong as I, if it *is* authentic. The primary difference, therefore, between the *Ariyasāvaka* and the *puthujjana* cannot be whether he regards this or that book (or passage) authentic, and others not, but simply *his open-mindedness towards anything claiming to be Dhamma-Vinaya* (Mahāpadesā, Dīgha 15). After all, our position is in no way different from that of the compilers of our texts, as they stand.

Please do not create a difference here. It should be clear now that I do not really mean to reject the passages under review, which is, exactly, why I consult you. (I beg you to forget my provoking statements.) And, also, I do have no idea to make *you* reject them, upon my word. It is possible, though not certain yet, that you are right, and I wrong. Therefore, do not let us approach the matter from the angle of authenticity please, which is a bar rather than an approach.

3/4. It appears to me now that the 'universal law' point of view at least has the advantage that *it does not exclude* (the 'pedagogical device' point of view, nor any other) that is why it is called so. I have made no attempt to invalidate your view, simply *because I see no reason for doing so*, quite to the contrary! Your fascinating statement that the *puthujjana*, on ceasing to be *puthujjana*, becomes *Arahat* (in due course), to me (though certainly not to many people), at last *is a basis* on which to discuss the position of the *sekha*, neither more nor less. And, as yet, you fortunately did not cut me off from such a discussion entirely; therefore I shall continue it.

It is not possible directly to translate the attitude of the mathematician (or any other scientist) towards his studies into the attitude of an individual towards the Buddha's Teaching, save perhaps in the case of the *puthujjana*. We have to be careful here if we want to avoid unnecessary differences. As I understand you, your argument seems to imply two different types of individuals, apart from the *puthujjana*, i.e. the *Dhammānusārī* and the *Saddhānusārī* on the one hand, and the *Sekha* (or *Arahat*) on the other.

Yes, to me, the Teaching does indeed *account* for everything (*paṭiccasamuppāda*), but it does not *concern* itself with everything, unlike science: it excludes, but *in order to* include (*Nibbāna*), that is why it is *atthasaṃhita*, what science fails to be. In this essential aspect, the Teaching differs from science, and, also, in that it has *quite different* axioms than science. In one aspect, however, both are alike, their axioms are self-evident. The Teaching, after all, is *ehi passa*!(*ka*). But please do not let us fall out over this either. Here, too, I rather include than that I exclude. I also admit that it is *not* self-evident, as I will have occasion to explain in the next paragraph.

For the moment, let me say this much. If I really approach the Buddha's Teaching, i.e. as a *Dhammānusārī* or *Saddhānusārī*, who are neither *puthujjanā* nor *Sekha*, I do demonstrate thereby *two* facts. Firstly, that *I do know already* (that I *can* know), and, secondly, that *I do not know* yet (what I *can* know). This is what is *saddhā*. In this way, I carefully would understand (if the comparison is relevant at all) the mathematician who sets out to master some branch of mathematics that he does not know yet. The other mathematician, however, (under the same assumption), who recognizes a false argument even without having ever come across it, simply because he has fully grasped the laws inherent in all mathematics, is none but the *Sekha* (or *Arahat*). (I have said already under para 2. what I consider the primary attitude of these individuals towards the Dhamma, as it has come down to us. The more essential points I shall now discuss, in some other context.) In this was, I assume *both*, namely, that the (intelligent does not apply, what should be clear) *puthujjana* (more correctly, *Dhammānusārī* and *Saddhānusārī*) does differ relatively *as well as* absolutely from the *Sekha*.

[Now I had to write already four pages without touching upon anything that really interests me. If I succeeded in dispelling the wrong impression I myself created, it shall be well. If not, I am not worried. Even if you choose to style me openly an 'intelligent *puthujjana*'—it only makes me smile. For I know by experience that highly intellectual men like you are dependent upon [illeg.], and that a lot of 'circumstantial evidence' is wanted to convince them, even on some level. I am more fortunate, because I am not dependent upon such evidence in the same way. And, therefore, my veneration for you is quite unshaken. That is why I am anxious that you should reply to what follows, rather than that to what preceded. But, of course, as you please.]

6. Your reference to Mūlapariyāya in connection with our argument whether or not the *Anāgāmī* is liable to *upādāna* is not relevant. The 24 (if I am right) items of that Sutta, one and all, are of an ontological nature (*loka-cintā*), but not so our question.

Apart from this, however, I can see some misunderstanding between us, which, probably, is due to my not having made clear my point sufficiently, though I did indicate it. I have made the following note on the whole question, please see whether you can perhaps agree on it. (By no means do I want to say that *knowledge* of the four truth is dependent upon *taṇhā*.)

*Identity of diṭṭhi and avijjā.* The mistaken tradition, that adds to the three *āsavā* of the Suttas a fourth (*diṭṭhāsava*), yet reflects a fact: *diṭṭhi* and *avijjā* are the same, at least from the angle of *āsava*. There is no *diṭṭhi* that is not *avijjā*, and there is no *avijjā* that is not *diṭṭhi*. *Sammādiṭṭhi*
M. 117 of the first degree (*puññabhāgiyā*) is *diṭṭhupādāna* for the fact that it is *puññabhāgiyā*. It is justified only as an equivalent to *micchādiṭṭhi*; in the face of *sammādiṭṭhi* of the second degree (*anāsavā*; note that only here *knowledge* of the four truths is implied), which is the *Dhamma-*

*cakkhu*, it is null and void. But again, *sammādiṭṭhi* of the second degree (*anāsavā*) can be styled so only in relation to *sammādiṭṭhi* of the first degree (*puññabhāgiyā*); in itself, it is not *diṭṭhi*, but *paññā*, or even *vijjā*. And it should be noticed that it is not *diṭṭhi*, but *these*, that overthrow the hierarchy of *avijjā*. *Diṭṭhi* can only pave the way to this end. Every *diṭṭhi*, and not only *micchādiṭṭhi* stands in relation to, and, therefore, *is*, *avijjā*. It ceases to be when *paññā* or *vijjā* arises, either temporarily and limitedly (the *Dhammacakkhu* of the *Sekha*), or, permanently and unlimitedly (as *vimutti* of the *Arahat*). (*Paññā* and *vijjā* occupy the same range; *vijjā* is *paññā vepullā*, amplified (not necessarily always), *paripūrī*, consummate must include the last of the *tevijjā*. (By the way, I do not understand why you say that the *Paññā-vimutta Arahat* does not have *arūpa-jhānā*; he does not have *aṭṭhavimokkhā*. The Venerable Sāriputta Thera was not *tevijja*, but *he* was *ubhato-bhāga-vimutta*[30], i.e. had the *aṭṭhavimokkhā*, including *arūpa-jhānā*), and *ṭhiti*, stable in time, permanent (my own expressions)).

may not have

Thus, the identity that I meant to establish of *diṭṭhi* and *avijjā* concerns *sammādiṭṭhi puññabhāgiyā*... and, of course, *micchādiṭṭhi*; these two are plainly *diṭṭhi*, and, at the same time, *diṭṭhupādāna*. The *Dhammacakkhu* is not involved, being *paññā*, and, consequently, the *Sekha* is *anupādāna* (temporally). There has never been a disagreement between us; only, why do you not admit the fact that is *time*? It is secondary, I know, but, nevertheless, there is no harm in admitting it, is there?

Since the *Anāgāmī* has *avijjā*, and you have agreed that *māna* and *udhacca* and *moha* (*avijjā* is *mahā-moha*), and since to have *avijjā* is to have *diṭṭhi*, the *Anāgāmī* is *saupādisesa* on account of *diṭṭhupādāna*, but, also, of course, on account of (*rūpa-*, *arūpa-*)*rāga*. The latter pertains to *taṇhā*. I cannot speak of *saupādisesa* other than in terms of *taṇhā* and *avijjā*, which are never one without the other, though, in the *Anāgāmī*, *taṇhā* no longer accounts as *upādāna*.

After I have made now such an effort to make clear what I mean, will you have the kindness of plainly stating (a) whether the *Dhammacakkhu* of the *Sekha* is temporal, and (b) whether not, *at other times*, he is liable to *diṭṭhi*, i.e. *diṭṭhupādāna* (as explained also in my other letter). Did you not say that day that the *Ariyasāvaka* does have a double vision? So what else can such a statement of yours mean but this, that he has *diṭṭhi* as well as *paññā*? I am intimately acquainted with the Kosambiya Sutta (M. 48), and, therefore, well aware that the *Diṭṭhisampanna* (=*paññavā*) has certain faculties that give him power to abandon *diṭṭhi* at will. But, yet, objectively, he remains what he is, i.e. not *Arahat*.

6a. *Diṭṭhi* as *sakkāyadiṭṭhi* or *attavāda*. For *diṭṭhi* (either *micchā-* or *sammā-*) to become *sakkāyadiṭṭhi* or *attavāda*, it requires a *marked* degree of *ayoniso manasikāra*, at which the *Sekha* never arrives. A *marked* degree of *manasikāra* to the *Sekha*, always is *yoniso*. But at *some* degree of *manasikāra* also the *Sekha* is *diṭṭhisampanna*, which is *paññā*. Now here something that was rankling in me ever since I read the relevant passage in your essay. At *some* degree of *manasikāra* if the *Sekha* is (*a*)*puññūpaga viññāṇa*, and you have agreed that also he can be so, he, evidently, is *diṭṭhigata*, and not *diṭṭhisampanna*. At the *marked* degree of *manasikāra*, however, it is the *Sekha* (or *Arahat*), and not the *puthujjana*, who is *āneñjūpaga viññāṇa*, namely, neither *puñña-* nor *apuñña*. Since the *puthujjana*'s *marked* degree of *manasikāra* is as much *diṭṭhigato* as any other degree, he always is (*a*)*puññūpaga viññāṇa*, and never *āneñjūpaga*, because this is dependent upon *paññā*, which is *adiṭṭhi*. The term *āneñja* I have never seen associated with the *puthujjana*, but always with either the *Sekha* or *Arahat*. I think even the Saṃyutta passage that you showed me that day only speaks of *puññūpaga viññāṇa*, does it not?

completely wrong

*Nāma-rūpa*. (i) This is clear. (*Pātubhava* would be *Erleben*, not *Erlebnis*, or *Erfahrung*.) (ii) The disagreement is due to failure to understand, what may mainly be my fault. *Nāma-rūpa-viññāṇa* stands or falls as a whole. I, precisely, said that. By the way, am I to assume that you hold that the four *upādānakkhandhā*, apart from *rūpa-*, pertain to *nāma*? I cannot imagine it, but it just strikes me that this is the accepted view, is it not? To me, this is as absurd as to hold that *paṭhigasamphassa* pertains to the five bases, and *adhivacanasamphassa* to the mind. You need make no remark on it if you do *not* hold this view, for there is no reason for me to assume it from your remarks, but I am not quite sure. It is clear, then, that experience and *pañcupādānakkhandhā* are one and the same thing. And you are quite right to say that it is *upādāna* from which I must start to untie the Gordian knot. However, I said exactly that. Only you may not have been able fully to grasp what I attribute to *phassa* (*nāma*). I said that *phassa* is *identical* with experience, and *phassa* is *sāsava saupādāna*. In other words, along with *phassa*, *upādāna* dissolves. In that way, *nāma* is the loose end. In your note on *phassa* I find absolutely nothing to object to; the ideas are quite familiar to me.

If, therefore, you agree on what immediately precedes, this question at least would be settled. (v) With (III, IV) I shall deal separately tomorrow. (vi) Though I agree on how you define the difference between *sati* and *manasikāra*, I am not at all sure what the exact meaning (in terms of Dhamma) would be of reflexion. This, however, along with your notion of intention, may have to be put off. (vii) I still expect that you will go through my 'tidy chart', no matter under what angle, if you cannot regard it as an approach to *rūpa*; I also have some more approaches in store. Do not be so unkind to me.

9. Regarding the use of Pāli I rather meant to say kindly to express yourself *in terms of the Dhamma*. The Pāli medium certainly is closest to it. I find it rather hard to go e.g. through that extract; I do not have the background for it. My sole interest, ever since, has been the Dhamma; I have forgotten all else, including mathematics. Since I also do most of my thinking in English, that medium, as such, is all right.

10. *Magga-Phala.*[31] At least a reasonable reply.[a] I am quite satisfied for the moment.

11. What you understand by immediate experience still remains doubtful. It belongs to the sphere that is hardly accessible to me, because I am not acquainted with it (cp 9). To some degree, I will touch upon it tomorrow.

12. Regarding writing to you. I have said what I had to say in the beginning. (Your earlier essay, long since, was lost in the post. But I would you to send me a copy if you still have one (occasionally).

xii a) In continuation of my previous remarks on the characteristic features of the five factors of *nāma* some remarks on *saññā*.

*Evam etaṃ yathābhūtam / kammaṃ passanti paṇḍitā*
*Paṭiccasamuppādadasā / kammavipākakovidā ...*[32] (8,iii).

Certainly, it did not escape me that you are averse from taking into account *vipāka*. But, just as in the case of the 'pedagogical device' point of view, it did not so far occur to me that you want to be *saccābhinivesa* and say '*idam saccaṃ mogham aññaṃ*'[33]. *Kammavipāka* is an essential key also to the understanding of *paṭiccasamuppāda*, and in this connection, does *not* belong to the *acinteyyāni*. I am afraid, if also further you will ignore my important note on *papañcasaññāsaṅkhā*, which is based on

a. This remark does not pertain to *your* replies; I mean it with reference to the rubbish that is generally accepted here.

Majjhima 18, one of the most important Suttas, you will have cut me off from any further discussion. It is true, of course, that one need not necessarily introduce this point in connection with *phassa* as viewed in Mahanidāna; however, if I choose to do so, there is no harm in it. I am not afraid of complicated ideas, so long as they are correct, and pertain to Dhamma.

(ii) (8,iv) In two sentences you have denied me a reply to what I am most interested in. Certainly, I cannot possibly expect you to do so much, and indeed you have taken a lot of trouble. I am disappointed only in view of your lengthy remarks in your first paragraphs.

Our disagreement on *nāma* as 'evaluation' of *rūpa* perhaps only is a seeming one. The matter was not sufficiently clear to me to be communicated. I shall refer here to the handwritten remarks on *rūpa* at the end of your previous letter, which seemed to me quite in agreement with how I look upon it. You have said that *rūpa* requires *nāma* to appear, and that, apart from appearing, it does not exists; it must be felt, perceived, intended, contacted, and viewed (please do not take these translations too serious; it should be clear what is meant, at least roughly). The definition of rūpa is the four *mahābhūtā* and *catunnaṃ mahābhūtānaṃ upādāya rūpaṃ*[34]. In this definition, strictly speaking, *nāma* is implied in exactly the same way than in Mahānidāna: *Adhivacanasamphassa* is *upādāna*, if you accept my view on *phassa* (8,ii,v.). This is no surprise, because the two passages define the same thing. Now you have said that *rūpa* is not *appearance*, but that which appears, i.e. the *mahābhūta*, is this correct? In that way, strictly speaking, it are the *mahābhūtā* that are felt, perceived, intended, contacted, and viewed, on account of *upādāna*. Now this is all what I meant by 'evaluating'; the *mahābhūtā* must be 'utilized' in these five ways for (an) experience. And this 'utilization', essentially, is *adhivacana*. The last possible relation to *adhivacana*, a relation to end relation, is the notion of *Nibbāna* as *anakkhāta*. And here the sublimest form of *cetanā*, as I see it, also is implied: *chandajāto anakkhāte / manasā ca phuṭo siyā / kāmesu ca appaṭibaddha-citto / Uddhaṃsoto ti vuccati*[35] (Dhp. 218). Thus, the five factors of *nāma*, in some way or other, are 'evaluation', or 'utilization', or whatever you like to name it, of the *mahābhūtā*. Do you agree on it in this manner?

(iii) But now I have to go one step further, and, thereby, return to a (i). Unfortunately, you have made no remark on *papañcasaññāsaṅkhā*; but I cannot possibly assume that you do not agree here. I repeat, the characteristics (*liṅgā*) that pertain to *nāma* and *rūpa* respectively, and involve *paṭigha-* and *adhivacana-samphassa* respectively, are nothing but *papañcasaññāsaṅkhā*, which is *vipāka*, as stated in Majjhima 18. A table is not perceived as a table because it *is* a table, but because it has been previously so diversified (*papañceti*). This goes to say that a table, or any other thing, is not *mahābhūtamaya*, but *saññāmaya*. Also here, as in the case of *phassa* (8,ii,v), you can perhaps see what I meant by saying that *nāma* is the loose end from which to start. For I can never attain *Nibbāna* by attempting to do away with the *mahābhūtā*. But I can cease 'utilizing' them, here as *saññā*; and they have no being apart from being *saññā*. *Saññā* abolishes the *mahābhūtā* in much the same way as *phassa* the I (*loka-atta*). Do you agree on this?

(iv) A few remarks to amplify my point.

*Iddhi*. If a table is perceived *as a table* not on account of its *being* a table, but on account of its being *papañcasaññāsaṅkhā*, there is no reason why I should not attempt taking it e.g. *as a chair*. If I succeed, it becomes *iddhi*, if not, *cittakkhepa*. Since, however, *iddhi* only is temporal (at most it lasts till the end of a *kappa*), the fact is not abolished that a table, *so long as it appears at all*, is perceived as a table, and not as a chair. *Iddhi* only exists as an ultimately unsuccessful revolution against this fact, and, what actually happens is a mere substitution of one *saññā* for the other, *on the same level* (*kāma-loka*). *Iddhi*, precisely, exists *pāṭihārī* to *kāma-saññā* (here sensory, not sensual perception), does not transcend it, and, therefore, is rejected.

*Nava anupubba-nirodhā*.[36] These of course, are of indefinitely much more importance, because they substitute *kāma-* for *rūpa-* and *rūpa-* for *arūpa-saññā*, and arrive, as *saññā-vedayita-nirodhā*, at *papañcasaññāsaṅkhā-nirodhā*, through *sikkhā*, based, however, on the same principle of *papañcasaññāsaṅkhā* as *vipāka*, here *phala*; *kamma* is *sikkhā*. There are other ways of transforming *saññā* (the sets of *saññā* in Dīgha 33, 34, and elsewhere), that do not involve *samādhi*. All that is found to the right hand of my 'tidy chart' [that] was an attempt to show and clarify what I have tried here to express on *saññā*, from the *samādhi* point of view.

This much as to *saññā*.

I can not remember ever to have written such a long letter, and to have made such an effort to be understood. This already has one advantage. The terrible intellectual problems that assailed me soon after coming in contact with you begin to vanish; once more, I begin to stand on my own feet, and am no longer concerned (much) about your reply, or whether you will reply at all. (If you prefer it, you can discontinue our discussion now.)

In deepest veneration,

V.

III. The last sentence of para II[37] refers to the 'Note on *phassa*', which, however, must have perished in the great flames. So I had better say something about it. The reason why consciousness tends to be associated with the body (*saviññāṇaka kāya*) is of less immediate interest to us since it is concerned with the *saḷāyatanāni*, and we are present discussing *pañcakkhandhā*; I shall therefore not discuss this aspect. What is of immediate interest is why consciousness is so frequently indentified as the subject. In the 'Note on *phassa*' there is this passage: '_____'.[38] The *puthujjana* thinks 'things are *mine* because I am, because I exist'. He takes the subject ('I') for granted, and if things are appropriated, that is because *he*, the subject, exists. The *diṭṭhisampanna* sees, however, that this is the wrong way round. He sees that the notion 'I am' arises *because* things (so long as there is any trace of *avijjā*) present themselves as 'mine'. This significance (or intention, or determination) 'mine' of 'for me' is, in a sense, a *negative* aspect of the thing (or phenomenon), since it simply *points to a subject*; and the *puthujjana*, not seeing impermanence, deceives himself into supposing that there actually exists a subject—self—independent of the object (which is merely the *positive* aspect of the phenomenon—that which is 'for me'. In this way it may be seen that the *puthujjana*'s experience, the *pañcupādānakkhandhā*, has a *negative* aspect (the subject) and a *positive* aspect (the object). But, as pointed out in para II, experience in general (the *arahat*'s as well as the *puthujjana*'s) also has a *negative* aspect (i.e. *viññāṇa*) and a *positive* aspect (i.e. *nāmarūpa*), and it is very easy for the *puthujjana* to superimpose these two *entirely different* divisions of negative and positive and equate subject = *viññāṇa* and object = *nāmarūpa*. But one must be careful, for, in fact, the division subject/object is not a simple negative/positive division. If it were, only the positive would appear (or be phenomenal) and the negative would simple not appear *at all*, it would simply not exist. But the subject is, in a sense, phenomenal, it is an *existing* of *phenomenal negative*, a *negative that appears*. The fact is that the intention or determination 'mine', pointing to a subject, is a complex structure involving *avijjā*. The subject is not simply negative in relation to the positive object; it is *master* over the object, and is thus a kind of positive negative, a master who does not appear but who, somehow or other, *exists*. (And for whom the *puthujjana* is constantly searching—in vain!). In this connexion here is a passage from the 'appendix to the Note on P.S.'[39]

[p. 46-47: slightly reduced reproduction of the above rough draft.]

II The last sentence of para II, like the [illegible] in the [illegible] flames, must have perished in the great flames. ~~So I had better comment upon it apart~~ So I had better say something about it. ~~To begin with~~ The reason why consciousness tends to be associated with the body (saviññāṇaka kāya) is of less immediate interest to us since it is concerned with the cakkhuyatana, and we are at present discussing paṭiccasamuppāda; so I shall therefore not discuss this aspect. What is of immediate interest is why consciousness is so frequently identified as the subject. In the 'Notes on Dhamma' there is this passage: '__________'. ~~The thing to note is that the notion 'I am' arises because things are 'mine', and not the other way round.~~ The puthujjana thinks 'things are mine because I am, because I exist'. He takes the subject ('I') for granted, and if things are appropriated, that is because it, the subject, exists. The diṭṭhisampanna sees, however, that this is the wrong way round. He sees that the notion 'I am' arises because things (so long as there is any trace of avijjā) present themselves as 'mine'. ~~I have already pointed out, in the p.s. essay~~ in the 'Notes on p.s.' ~~that~~ ~~this significance 'mine' or 'for me' is [illegible] or intention, as determining the thing~~ This significance (or intention, or determination) 'mine' or 'for me' is, in a sense, a into supposing that there actually exists a subject (independent of the object (which is merely the positive aspect of the phenomenon &c. – that which is 'for me'). In this way it may be seen that the puthujjana's experience, the pañcupādānakkhandhā, has a negative aspect (the subject) and a positive aspect (the object). But, as pointed out in para. 11, experience in general (the arahat's as well as the puthujjana's) also has a negative aspect (i.e. viññāṇa) and a positive aspect (i.e. nāmarūpa), and it is very easy for the puthujjana to superimpose these two entirely different divisions of negative and positive and equate subject = viññāṇa and object = nāmarūpa. But we must be careful; for, in fact, the division subject/object is not a simple negative/positive division. If it were, only the positive would appear (or be phenomenal) and the negative would simply not appear at all – it would simply not exist. But the subject is, in a sense, phenomenal; it is an existing or phenomenal negative, a negative that appears. The fact that the reflexive determination 'mine', points to a subject, is a complex structure involving avijjā. The apparent "subject" is not simply a negative in relation to the positive "object": it is master over the object, and is thus a kind of positive negative, a master who does not appear but who, somehow or other, exists. In this connexion, here is a passage from the 'Appendix to the Notes P.S.' (And for whom the puthujjana is constantly searching – in vain!).

**[SV. 7]** **16 December 1961**

Parts (save only the last two sentences) of your note 2 on *Note on Phassa*[40] aroused many doubts at first sight. The matter, however, as I see it, has no bearing on your concept of *phassa*, on which I fully agree. Rather, it pertains to *saññā* (*nānatta*).

You have made the multiplicity of (visual) experience dependent on the use of two eyes (instead of only one). Now it is not clear what you mean by multiplicity. You seem to stress that it is between the *ajjhattikāyatana* and the *bāhirāyatana*. The fact is, however, that *nānatta*, in the *kāma-loka*, pertains to *each āyatana*, and not to the duality of experience as such, which is duality, and not multiplicity.

The fleshly eye, whether one or two, has nothing to do with either. The beings of the *rūpa-* and *arūpa-loka* do not have fleshly eyes, yet there is in their experience both, duality and multiplicity (the latter is not in the *rūpa-loka*).

Kindly clear this point please.

Respectfully,

V.

**[SV. 8]** **17 December 61**

Dear Bhante,

If there is anything in my earlier letter that is inappropriate, I beg you to forgive me, and, also—please do not reply to it. I am inwardly torn, that is why I repeatedly contradicted myself as to whether or not to write. I am sorry for it.

After dawn gradually came upon me of what you are, and what you represent, I know that it is only humility that befits me, and not argument.

I need time to digest the new phenomenon in my life that is you, especially, since it presents itself as a terrible conflict. On the one hand, you are having an absolutely controlling influence over me—I am no longer the same, from the time that I first saw you—but not intellectually. There are faint shadows of *avijjā*, if I may say this, attendant upon you, which however, under these circumstances, prove to be quite consuming to me, out of all proportion. If I do not cease facing this conflict that you are to me, by arguing with you, I can no longer find any peace at all.

I am extremely sorry for disturbing you by telling all this. I knew intuitively that my relations to you had to end where they began, but, unfortunately, a letter or yours, almost against my will, came into my hands afterwards and entailed further correspondence. You need not worry. I can find myself again. This is not the first, but the second, time that I see myself confronted with a conflict of this order. I must become independent now, that is all.

In deepest veneration,

V.

**[SV. 9]** **24 December 1961**

Thank you very much for your letter *hitūnkampī* of the 19th. Instant. I received it yesterday, along with your addition to 'Note on *Phassa*'. Since it does not seem to be my 'fate' to succeed in cutting myself away from you, on the level of discussion (your delivery of letters seems to be rather unregular), I had better try to become more reasonable, to myself as well as to you, in accordance with the saying in German '*was mich nicht umwirft, macht mich starker—what does not overthrow me, makes me stronger*'. Also, like you, I see the 'natural death' of our correspondence quite close at hand. For it is clear enough now that the real question is that of *pañc(upādāna-k)khandhā*, and there are only a few more points that I have not yet fully exhausted, so as to see clearly for myself our differences. By your addition on *phassa*, as you are aware, you have done nothing but consistently pursued your view—leaving no hole for me whatsoever to slip through. But I consider your consistency an advantage rather than a disadvantage; it shortens my way. It is quite clear to me that, for ever, I will be the foolish ripple at the feet of a solid rock—I do not, and never did, hope to shake you; rather, I hope to calm down before long myself. Like last time, I shall make my remarks in the succession of your letter.

Simply because of my deep veneration for you and the bearing it has on this very correspondence of ours, a few personal remarks will perhaps not be altogether out of place, quite irrespective, of course, of what you will take them for. From the time that the Bhagavā's Teaching became the guiding star in my life (1949) I have never in any conceivable form, and space of time, entertained the idea of *punabbhava*; the whole of my conscious and subconscious experience is entirely free from the element 'future'—I perceive absolutely nothing beyond this life. With the same definiteness I can also state the same thing positively, but it should not be necessary. What happened to me after coming in contact with you is this. (I am afraid I will hardly be able to convey it even approximately. But I will try my best—after the manner of the waste-paper-basket-principle.) I had found, so to speak, the correct 'formula' (in 49), but, in a sense, I did not really positively put it to the test; it was there, but not looked at. In that sense, you are perhaps not so much in the wrong to say that I am sterile. (I want to dwell upon this matter at some length because it will throw light on my whole outlook, which, in this particular point,

i.e. to get rid of it even if it is not to be understood

differs most widely from yours. Our whole discussion, if it is ever to be continued, rests upon an understanding of this difference.) My aptitude to abstract thought, thus, would seem a weakness rather than a strength. However, and this is now the point, it cannot be taken into account separately, if the matter is to be understood. For, on the other hand, I am a 'visionary' type; a vision, here in the 'mystical' sense, but also an ordinary visual experience, has the same hold on me as an abstract idea. And, in fact, the two decisive religious experiences that I distinguish so far (in 49 and now) are inseparably both. Strictly speaking, also the ideas I communicate are not arrived at by way of systematic thought; for me, everything essentially is a seeing and, secondarily, a telling. And you are quite right to say that I care little for being understood, though not here. From this angle it is to be explained why my way of writing seems so elliptical, and why too many things come out at once. But, also, my fondness for schemes is to be explained in this way. I have an unquenchable desire to visualise my ideas (or: ideals), however absurd this may appear. (By the way, I was a draftsman, and the branch of higher mathematics that I acquired some knowledge of was spherical Euclids (if this is the right term in English). But now the more important thing—vision of the individual. I have repeatedly indicated to you that I find myself intimately involved with others, and you did perhaps realize the fact by yourself in between. It is therefore no surprise that also my religious experiences referred to above are bound up with an individual. And here I shall return to where I started from. When I came to see you in Polgasduwa the discussion only was a pretence; all that I really cared for was to visualize your inner face. Since I succeeded, beyond expectation, and arrived at a second turning-point of my life, it was only natural that the 'formula', too, suddenly, and because of our disagreements on essential points, rendered itself conspicuous, and, at the a time where I least of all expected it, forced itself upon me for reconsideration. This is conflict, and not so much intellectual upheaval, though these are only names.

Since you always say that you fail to grasp my ideas, what I mean by 'formula', essentially, is that there is no difference between *pañcakkhandhā* and *pañc'upādānakkhandhā*. And I can see already fairly clearly that I am quite unshaken where this is concerned. (But I hope this will
xii not be a hindrance for you to do your best to 'refute' me.) But, unlike you, I am unshaken not in the sense of being 'intransigent' on any matter

whatsoever; I am not concerned with views; I am concerned with *Arahattā* here and now, and if you can prove the difference *pañc(upādānak)-khandhā* I cannot possibly fail to grasp it. It should be noticed, once and for all, that I may fail in following you, if I do not find it worthwhile to make the necessary effort, but not if I do make such an effort—and it is unnecessary to say that indeed I would do so (within the limits of strict Dhamma, of course).

prove?

I have made up my mind to add another page or so on this matter in order to make my position as clear as possible (to myself). When I said that I succeeded in visualizing your inner face, I mean to say the very opposite of what it seemingly stands for. I do not conceive in terms of objectivity, and, consequently, lay no claim on having understood you. I have understood you for what you are *to me*, and, apart from that, I am not concerned with any object whatsoever. The same thing, more precisely, I have understood you what you are to me in relation to what most immediately concerns me—*Arahattā*. And in that I did so, I was greatly shaken, for this experience directly corresponds to what happened in 49: at that time, I saw the Dhamma—now, the *Arahat*. My vision of you, thus, is strictly subjective in two ways; it remains below you, and it goes beyond you. In the first place, I do not at all fathom you. I am not only the foolish ripple at the feet of a solid rock, if I try it, but, rather, I become restless as the ocean itself. Best I could perhaps express what you are to me, from this angle, paradoxically, which, again, is the language of the 'visionary', the 'mystic', in particular, the Chinese (Lao tzu, in its purest form). I would, however, never expect of *you* to understand it, though I must confess that it is my domain proper where communication is concerned—while it takes me great pains to be explicit like this. By far more essential, however, is the other aspect, though not to be separated from the first: I have seen in you the *Arahat*, and this was all that was needed to end my 'sterility'. The correspondence of ours, altogether, is a mere troublesome appendage, which, however, I must face bravely, in order to shorten my way. Even if you would be able to prove that my 'formula' is wrong, it does not alter things. Quite on the contrary; since I am not concerned with views, but with *Arahattā*, it would only bring me closer to it. Thus, in whatever way I look at it—what does not overthrow me makes me stronger—: my relation to you has no other significance than to make me conscious of my own powers.

You always say that I understand (which really means misunderstand, as I found out) things as they fit in with my scheme of thoughts. Well, also in this matter, I can do nothing. You are not a 'visionary'; you arrive at your conclusions by way of orderly thought, or 'circumstantial evidence', and that takes *time*—the thing you most bitterly deny. There is on comfort only, that is why I did not give up wrestling with you, your absolute consistency. If not for that, long since I would have abandoned our correspondence, but I have got used to expecting the unexpected from you.

2. *Saupādisesa nibbānadhātu*. What was said in the foregoing pages may suffice for the time being, i.e. I do see the problem just as you say. I want first to prepare the ground for a direct discussion of this matter, if it ever should come to it, by dealing with the question of *kamma/kammavipāka* below.

3. I have some ideas on the disctinction between the *satta puggalā* and the *aṭṭha puggalā*. The question is of interest, since, however, I would have to look at the passages referred to by you, as well as at one that I have in view, I cannot deal with it here, because my books are away, and I do not go out these days.

4. The question whether *diṭṭhupādāna* is to be associated with the *Anāgāmī* is absolutely exhausted. As in the case of *phassa*, consistently, you hold your ground. Really, the severity of your argument makes me sigh, but, with the best will, I cannot bring myself to agree with you. Regarding your quotation in your Paṭiccasamuppāda on *loka-cintā*, or whatever it may be called, I ruled out Mūlapariyāya only with regard to the question of the Anāgāmī, which I hold is not *ṭhapanīya*, that is all.

5. Thanks for pointing out to me the passage on *ānañjūpaga viññāṇa* (your essay, too, is not here; someone is reading it). I will make further study of *ānañja*. It was in our conversation that you had admitted that also the *Ariyasāvaka* can be *(a)puññūpaga*, not in the essay.

6. —.—

7. I do not agree on your interpretation of that Suttanipāta passage. I am, on principle, disinclined to take any statement of the Bhagavā in a double sense; so e.g. *saupādisesā* (in the context of *Anāgāmitā* and *nibbānadhātu*), and your quotation *yaṃ kiñci vedayitaṃ taṃ dukkhasmin ti*[41], which I find sufficiently proved wrong in the Majjhima (one of the Kammavibhaṅga Suttas?), though, in the case of the latter, I am still more uncertain whether I can stick to my principle, since I do not know well enough in what context it occurred, in the Saṃyutta. But, in the case

quote Nid. Saṃy. iv,2

of *paṭiccasamuppādadasā kammavipākakovidā*[42] of Sn, I hold that it is meant in an absolute sense, simply because I do not see such obstacles as you see to combine the two views,[a] rather, I believe that they are one and the same thing. Though I can certainly understand what you attach to *akālika*, I can not share your interpretation of *paṭiccasamupāda*, excluding all notion of time, as being the *only* one. I shall tomorrow try to pursue the matter from the viewpoint of *saññā*, and, thereby, make the probably last attempt to come to an understanding with you (even though I have no hope whatsoever to succeed).

9. *Saññā.* (a) To be sure, the *ajjhattikāyatanāni*, being *indriyāni*, are not identical with the sense organs that correspond to them, which, in fact, are *bāhirāyatanāni*. Thus, subject and object are absolute. (If the sense-organ were identical with *ajjhattikāyatanāni* subject and object would be interchangeable, what your second note on 'Note on *Phassa*' seems to mean. I do not regard this matter quite so harmless as you make it appear in reply to my postcard. But if you really mean it, I am not interested in it, because it remains on the surface.) (b) I do hold now that both *āyatanā* are *vipāka*, for the simple reason that the *bāhirāyatanā* are *saññākāyā*, and that every *saññā* is *papañcasaññāsaṅkhā*. (c) From this it is clear already that the notion of *attā*, which you have said *tends* to be superimposed on the *ajjhattikāyatanāna*[b] (the subject), I hold to be superimposed on the either, equally. The fact that it gets superimposed at all is the deception that is *phassa*, and, at the same time, *kamma* (*nava*). (d) I am afraid in this connexion I have to refer you to the *satta viññāṇaṭṭhitiyo*, the first four. Irrespective of *nānatta* and *ekatta* as such, the very fact that *kāya* (*ajjhattikāyatanāna*, the subject), and *saññā* (*bāhirāyatanam*, the object) is described as being experienced by these *sattā nānattaṃ ekattaṃ*, which in itself is *saññā*, to me, is evidence that I am correct as to (b) and (c).[c]

Since you might find it impossible to follow this line of argument, I will try something else. (And indeed the situation could be saved if you could accept it.) You say that *paṭiccasamupāda* is a principle and not

---

a. or interpret them in some other way

b. *saññā-paṭicca cetana = vipāka-paṭicca kammaṃ*

c. I can quote Sn passages to show relation between *nāma-rūpa* and *papañca*, but no doubt, you are better acquainted with them than myself.

simply a name for the series. That is certainly so, and I quite agree on it. I also understand and agree that *paṭiccasamupāda*, being the most essential part of the Teaching, must be kept free from all temporal notions. Further, you are quite right to say that the inversion suggested by you does not in any way help me to understand *paṭiccasamupāda*. But here now I have to say that this is not the *only* inversion: it is the understanding of *papañcasaññāsaṅkhā*, on which I have made sufficient remarks to be commented upon, and to which I shall not add here, which leaves *paṭiccasamupāda akālika*, without excluding *kamma/vipāka*.[a] And this is the only view on *kamma/vipāka* I am interested in, and keenly.

8. It is clear now that *everything* in our discussion depends on *nāma-rūpa/viññāṇa*. More than ever before, I am curious to know your views. To avoid the various difficulties connected with communicating them, I would suggest this. Can you not kindly try to translate your ideas, *to the degree that I have touched upon it*, into terms of Dhamma, and so communicate them by degrees?[b] I am most anxious to know, and that is really all I care for, how you get round the difficulty of objectivity when all *dhammā* (so long as there is *avijjā*) are misconceived, i.e. how can I hope to go beyond subjectivity without abandoning objectivity? Did you not say that the world and I are strictly correlative?

In deepest veneration,

V.

---

a. *Nava anupubbanirodhā sikkhā = kamma; phala (vimutti) = vipāka*

b. Generally you tend to say more than what is needed.

**[SV. 10]** **26 December 1961**

I find it quite impossible not to associate *nāma-rūpa* with *papañca* (*saññāsaṅkhā*). I give you below the relevant Suttanipāta passages referred to in my letter.

[530] *Anuvicca papañca-nāmarūpaṃ*
*Ajjhattaṃ bahiddhā ca rogamūlaṃ:*
*Sabbarogamūla bandhanā pamutto*
*Anuvidito tādi pavuccate tathattā.*[43]

Still more here, in support of my conception *rūpa* = *saññā*:

[874] *Na saññasaññī na visaññasaññī*
*No pi asaññī na vibhūto saññī:*
*Evaṃ same tassa vibhoti rūpaṃ*
*Saññānidānā hi papañcasaṅkhā.*[44]

Here more the general importance of *papañca*:

[916] *Mūlaṃ papañcasaṅkhāyā*
*Manta asmīti sabbam uparundhe*
*Yā kāci taṇhā ajjhataṃ*
*Tāsaṃ vinayā sadā sato sikkhe.*[45]

Respectfully,

V.

**[SV. 11] 27 December 1961**

Dear Bhante,

In between I was able to check the references on *Dhammānusārī* etc. I made enclosed notes[1] on the whole question of the *Ariyasāvaka*, as related to final deliverance. As I said already, this is one of the matters that really interests me, and I see none apart from you who check this note of mine. Will you kindly do so, occasionally? If this is less troublesome to you, you can make remarks directly on it, on the reverse, or whatever you please. (I even prefer it, because I have no copy of it.)

I also referred to A.iii,413, which you quoted in support of your interpretation of Suttanapāta 653. Even before referring to it in the Aṅguttara, merely from your letter, I saw already that this passage fits in perfectly well with how *I* look upon it. But, of course, *your* interpretation is *included*, and most comfortably, not excluded. To me, this is nothing but *paṭiccasamupāda* context, the whole Sutta. *Vohāra* as *vipāka* is nothing but what I tried to explain in my latest notes on *saññā*, especially, in my reference to *satta viññāṇaṭṭhitiyo*, or in an universal context, in my *rūpa*-chart (*vohārā* = *kāyā*).[2]

In deepest veneration,

V.

---

1. Returned to Sister V., duly annotated.
2. A. IV, 123 (A.ii,126-8): 'Both formerly and now, bhikkhus, it is just suffering I declare and the cessation of suffering.'

**[L. 148/158] 27 December 1961**

Dear Upāsikā,

I have indicated the points of difference between us on this question of the *ariyapuggalā*, and I do not have any doubt that I am right. But if you can give me a Sutta text that clearly shows that I am mistaken I shall not be greatly worried. It is not within my powers to check for myself that all four (or eight) stages are necessarily gone through by all who eventually attain *arahattā*, nor can I know for myself that there are just four (or eight) stages, no more and no less. And whether or not a *sotāpanna* is or is not to be called *kāyasakkhī*, *diṭṭhipatto*, or *saddhāvimutto* is, after all, a question of terminology rather than anything else. For all these matters I rely on the Buddha (or the Suttas), since I cannot know them for myself; and if it is pointed out to me that I have misunderstood the Suttas, I am prepared to reconsider my views on this matter. Nothing of any great importance depends upon a person's knowing about the various kinds of *ariyasāvakā*: what *is* of importance is that he should become one of them—the rest will follow as a matter of course.

By way of contrast, I remember that a few years ago (at the Hermitage) the question arose whether or not *viññāṇa* is included in *nāma*, and at that time I said in public that if anyone were to show me a Sutta where *viññāṇa* definitely was included in *nāma* I should be extremely upset. (Fortunately nobody did.) The reason for my statement was that as a result of an examination of my own experience (guided also by certain outside philosophers) I had come to the conclusion that it was quite wrong to include *viññāṇa* in *nāma*; this was (and is) a matter wherein I could (by reflexive experience) know for myself what was right and what was wrong; and a Sutta in direct contradiction to my own experience would have been most disturbing.

Perhaps you will see from this distinction that I have made (between what I *can* know for myself at the present time and what I can *not* know) why it is that I am unable to make any useful comment on your 'tidy chart' of *rūpa*. Nearly all of it is quite beyond my present experience and nothing I could say would be anything more valuable than a discussion of certain words. And the same applies, generally, to any argument based upon etymology and Sutta usage. At best I can only indicate Suttas to complete or to correct your scheme. (Thus, I can say that you may find the answer to your question 'Where do the four *jhānas* belong?' in A. IV, 123 & 124.)

With best wishes,

Ñāṇavīra

**[SV. 12] 6 January 1962**

Dear Bhante,

You have written me a most sensitive and responsive letter, for which I am extremely grateful to you. I do not think and never did, that there is much of a resemblance in my correspondence with you and yours with the Venerable Ñāṇamoli—not only do I understand myself better at every turn, I also feel better *understood*. And, though the first thing certainly is of greater importance, the latter is by no means inessential, for had you not succeeded in understanding me better, you could not possibly go a long way to becalm me; as in fact, you do. Thus, I may say that, in the main at least, my purpose in writing to you is achieved already; what follows only is to round off matters.

It is one of the absurdities you consist of (in my experience) that you are not a religious person. If I take a deep breath, however—as it often happens when I think of you—I can grasp it. For you, there is no need to be religious, because you represent what religion itself rests upon—saintliness. The rest of men, necessarily, has no other way then to be religious, in order to follow such as you are—which is no easy thing, and, at times, may lead to extremes.

2. I came to see clearly now for myself that the perplexity much of your argumentation arouses in me is almost entirely bound up with the phenomenon *Arahat*, and does probably not concern *pañcakkhandhā*
as such. If the *Arahat* (and *Sekha*, who, to you, essentially is *Arahat*) X
were excluded, there would probably be no much of a difficulty. But this is mere theory (quite so as if this was possible!).

The only inconsistency I could charge you with—though I do not mean to—which, however, is just the one that matters (as if it could be otherwise!) is this. Rigorously, you exclude the *Sekha* from *paṭiccasamupāda* X
*anuloma*, for the *Arahat*, however, whom you apparently hold *paṭiloma*, X
you allow a 'but' and 'when', which, strictly speaking, really is a putting X
him back to *paṭiccasamupāda anuloma*—there is no conceivable *outside* this context. But what I mean is this (it appeared settled in our talk at Polgasduwa): the *Arahat* is as much appropriated to the *pañc'upādānakkhandhā* (i.e. to *paṭiccasamupāda anuloma*) that *I* am liable to than any other phenomenon in my experience, and there is no 'but' and 'when' whatsoever that is not plainly *myself*. Hence, the *Arahat is taboo*.

Though is would be silly to offer any objections to *how you* describe the *Arahat* (on the one hand, I love to hear it!) nevertheless, there is in me an insurmountable resistance *that* he should be described—in terms other than strictly negatively to *pañc'upādānakkhandhā*. Thus, I can say of him e.g. that he is *khīṇāsavā*, *akataññū*, *pāragū*, *visaṃyutta*, *katakicca*, *pannabhāro*, *anupādāya parinibbuta*, *antimasārīra*, *nirūpadhī*, *āneñja*[46], etc. etc., and then, I (personally) do not have a good chance of really seeing *him*, and not *me*. Can you understand what I mean? I get greatly disconcerted when you describe him 'as such'; it is extremely difficult for me to see e.g. that objects do have any significance apart from being 'mine' (as you always emphasize); I can not at all regard it as settled that e.g. the robe offers itself to be worn (by *himself*, that is) also to the *Arahat*. As I see it, the *Arahat* as well as the robe—both are *mine*. It is *myself* who is unable to see any other relation between the *Arahat* and the robe, except that it is to be worn by him (i.e. is *his*)—so long as these things *appear to me* (i.e. are *paṭiccasamupāda anuloma*, or, within *pañc'upādānakkhandhā*). I shall touch upon this matter again below.

not 'by him-self'

no

However, I do not say this to contradict you. I only would like you to understand what is *my* position also in this matter. I know now, and, in so far am appeased, that *yours* is different. You are indefinitely much closer to the *Arahat* than myself, and, therefore, *can afford* looking at him in any way. In fact, is not your whole being (as I see it) an approximation to *Arahattā*? While mine *consists in* a denial of it! For me, there is no approximation; my whole nature is an 'either-or'—I have never felt it so sorely as now. And this probably also is the last word on *pañcakkhandhā*. For you, the question is settled (whether rightly or wrongly I have never felt called upon to decide), for me, however, it would be *wrong* if it were—like previously! I would not have seen the *Arahat* if it could ever be settled again; I rather will suffer the intellectual discrepancy I am in now, than have that question settled. I find myself rather in the position of the bhikkhu from the Kevaddha Sutta[47].

3. I must indeed say that I have a very different notion of *papañcasaññāsaṅkhā* than you; it is a magical word to me, if I may use this expression—as all-including as to you reflexion. Majjhima 18 appears to me much more involved than what you take it for. However, it is clear now, that our difference is entirely dependent upon our attitude towards *kamma* and *kammavipāka*, which, to me, is immediately accessible, and, hence, plainly inseparable from my every theme of thought. The

more do I appreciate that you have made up your mind to comment on it at all, and, in particular, it is kind of you to indicate to me the line of thought that *you* have followed, involving no such temporal notions as these. It was, however, never hidden from me, for the simple reason that it is by no means alien to me, nor the bearing it has on your own spiritual development. In fact, it is this very way of thinking that fascinated me in your essays, and for which I say that I do not at all fathom you. Not only that I could never develop such an admirable and powerful intellectual instrument by myself. I could not even make it my own if it were fully known to me. However, I can appreciate it, so as to see that it is probably quite capable of abolishing subjectivity, or objectivity, it comes to the same. So far, it was most disturbing to me that you seemed to allow anything in experience to be 'given' or 'gratuitous' without identifying it with *vipāka*, and you hardly can succeed dispelling my suspicion; but, of course, I know too little of your ideas, especially also your notion of *rūpa*, as to come to a conclusion. On the whole, I need *more time* to understand you. quote Vedanā Saṃy. 21

At any rate, for the time being at least, I am not able to make a significant distinction between appropriated and mere teleological experience; they are, to me, inseparably on and the same, as already indicated. If I am pressed to designate the *Arahat*'s experience as such, all I can say is that I attribute everything in it to *kammavipāka—indriyāni*, *āyu*, and *usmā*—when these persist, experience functions automatically, and the *Arahat*, thus, becomes accessible to my own experience; and I am at an absolute loss to define him other than in terms of my own experience, which, however, I know is *sāsavā*, whilst his is *not*. Thus, the *Arahat*'s supposed way of experience converges with mine, and I dare not say which is whose.

If you find that there is anything wrong in my attitude, please do not fail to point it out to me.

4. I became aware of it already by myself that my remarks on *ajjhattikā* and *bāhirā āyatanā* would be unintelligible to you. But, though I had made the note you kindly may find enclosed already, it is only after closely attending to what you say in your last letter that I begin to understand what you are really concerned with. It is this concern that is quite alien to me. If you ask *me*, I do not at all regard my body *ajjhattika*, and, hence, such an idea is accessible to me only in theory, especially as represented in the passage quoted by you (Nidāna Saṃyutta

ii,9). Apart from the note mentioned, the following seems to be necessary to make things clear.

If I said that the notion of self gets superimposed on both *āyatanā* (*ajjhattika* and *bāhira*), I meant to say nothing but this: *Yaṃ kiñci rūpaṃ* (etc.) *atītānāgata paccuppannaṃ ajjhattaṃ vā bahiddhā vā oḷārikaṃ vā sukhumaṃ vā hīnaṃ vā paṇītaṃ vā yaṃ dūra santike vā sabbaṃ rūpaṃ: etaṃ mama eso 'haṃ asmī eso me attāti.*[48] I perceive a clear distinction between the subject—as opposed or correlative to the object—and the inherent subjection or appropriation (your expression) of *everything*, exactly as in the phrase quoted, including the two *āyatanā* (the subject and object). Is there anything strange in it?

(ii) I had stressed in my remarks last time that the *indriya* carefully has to be distinguished from the sense-organ that corresponds to it; from my note you will see that I go so far as to say that the sense-organ is *bāhira*. Once more, you will see that my notions are rather involved. I wonder whether you will find it possible to see my meaning.

5. Though you have declined dealing with the question of *Anāgāmītā* and *diṭṭhupādāna* any further, I have to make the following notes on it. (i) In *avijjāgato yaṃ bhikkhave purisapuggalo puññañ ce ... āneñjañ ce saṅkhāraṃ abhisaṅkharoti āneñjūpagaṃ hoti viññāṇaṃ*, *avijjāgato*[49] stands for *diṭṭhigāta* (*avijjā* = *diṭṭhi*), and, thus, includes the *Sekha* (*Anāgāmī*). The Aneñjasappya Sutta (M.ii,262) establishes that the *Ariyasāvaka* can be *āneñjūpaga viññāṇa*. But, apart from this, I still hold that the *puthujjana* does not at all arrive at *āneñjūpaga viññāṇa*; the Sutta mentioned speaks in this connection of the *Ariyasāvaka*. But, curiously enough, the *Ariyasāvaka* (and in so far I was wrong) arrives at it not as *diṭṭhisampanna* but as *diṭṭhigata*, for otherwise it could not say *paññāya vā adhimuccati*[50]. Thus, I have no difficulties in understanding your Saṃyutta passage in my own way—whether you agree or not.

(ii) What about the following passage (M.ii,264f)? *Idh'Ānanda bhikkhu evaṃ paṭipanno hoti No c'assa no ca me siyā ... upekhaṃ paṭilabhati. So taṃ upekhaṃ abhinandati abhivadati ajjhosāya tiṭṭhati. Tassa taṃ upekhaṃ abhinandato ... taṃ nissitaṃ hoti viññāṇaṃ tad upādānaṃ. Sa-upādāno Ānanda bhikkhu na parinibbāyatīti.—Kahaṃ pana so bhante bhikkhu upādiyamāno upādiyatīti? Nevasaññānāsaññāyatanaṃ Ānandāti ...* (the rest is interesting also in connection with your notion of *sakkāya*) *Idh'Ānanda ariyasāvako iti paṭisañcikkhati Ye ca diṭṭhadhammikā kāmā ..., yā ca nevasaññānāsaññāyatanasaññā, esa sakkāyo yāvatā sakkāyo etaṃ amataṃ yadidaṃ anupādā cittassa vimokkho...*[51]

In deepest veneretion,

V.

SAḶĀYATANA—PHASSA (a sketch) [*Correlation of attā and loka*]
(a) *Cakkhundriya. Maṃsa-cakkhu* (the rest accordingly)

In ordinary sensory experience the *cakkhundriya*, which is *ajjhatikāyatana*, is held to be identical with the *maṃsa-cakkhu*, which, however, really is *bāhirāyatana*. In ordinary sensory experience it is plainly impossible to escape the deception *cakkhundriya* = *maṃsa-cakkhu*, because the *cakkhundriya* is inconceivable apart from the *maṃsa-cakkhu*—they are bound up to each other, and do not go beyond each other. Thus, the body, being really *part of the object*, becomes subject, and the *rest* of the *bāhirāyatana* the object [and there takes place a *constriction* of experience, which, primarily, is felt as a *discrepancy* of subject and object, and, hence, *dukkha*.]

(b) *Cakkhundriya. Dibba-cakkhu* (the rest accordingly, so far as it applies)

But also in sensory experience involving *samādhi* the *indriya* comes to be identified with the *bāhirāyatana*, only in some other way. (i) If the *dibba-cakkhu* has no particular location to be taken *ajjhattaṃ*, i.e. is altogether unlike the *maṃsa-cakkhu*, the *bāhirāyatana* comes to be identified with it as such; (ii) if it does have a location in some form or other, resembling thus the *maṃsa-cakkhu*, a corresponding extent of the *bāhirāyatana* comes to be identified with it—just as in ordinary sensory experience only less limitedly. In the first case, the *dibba-cakkhu* is boundless (*appamāna*)—a convergence of *indriya* and *bāhirāyatana*—otherwise, more or less like the *maṃsa-cakkhu*, limited (*paritta*). This goes to say, that also the *dibba-cakkhu*, though either altogether, or more or less, free from the limitations of the *maṃsa-cakkhu* (which is limitation in *degree*), nevertheless, is entirely bound up with, and inconceivable apart from, the *bāhirāyatana* that *corresponds* to it, and, thus, essentially like the *maṃsa-cakkhu*, in so far is restricted. [Note, however, that this restriction, in the case of convergence, no longer is restriction in degree, but is absolute, i.e. is bound up with sensory experience as such. There is, however, experience of an altogether different type (*arūpa-loka*).] In other words, if in ordinary experience *part* of the object (i.e. the body) becomes subject, in sensory experience involving *samādhi* the object as such tends to become subject [and there takes place a *widening* of experience, which, primarily, is felt as a *merging* of subject and object, and, hence, *sukha*.]

(c) *Paññā-cakkhu* (= *Dhamma-Cakkhu*)

(i) Now, what does this mean? It is clear from the two types of experience discussed (which include every possible form of *sensory* experience) that sensory experience is determined for what it is—i.e. *dukkha* = *paritta*, or *sukha* = *appamāna*, or any degree between the two—by an *autonomous correspondence* of the two *āyatanā* (or correlation of self and world—dependent, however, as such, upon the *indriyā* (i.e. *saḷāyatana*). The *bāhirāyatana* are purely secondary to the *indriyā*, and given along with them. In this way it comes to be seen that the notion *Etaṃ mama eso 'haṃ asmi eso me attāti*[52] does get superimposed on *both āyatanā equally*, for the *indriyā*, *being subject*, *bring into subjection* the *object*, directly as *kāya*, and indirectly as *saññā* (*papañcasaññasaṅkhā*).

(ii) But, of course, though *saḷāyatana* determines experience for *what* it is, it is *phassa* that determines it for *that* it is at all. *Phassa*, now, comes to be when there is presence of object to subject, which is nothing but presence of *bāhirāyatana* to *ajjhattikāyatana*. Since, however, the former inherently is appropriated to the latter, *phassa* simply is dependent upon *saḷāyatana*. Or, to say the same thing in a different way, *saḷāyatana*, being essentially *identity* of the two *āyatanā*, gives rise to *phassa*, because it appears as being essentially *diversity* (i.e. *duality*). Thus, though *phassa* is not *between* the two *āyatanā*, it is also not *apart* from them, for *phassa* is dependent on duality, and there is no other duality than that of subject and object.

[L. 149/159] 10 January 1962

Dear Upāsikā,

1. It is going too far to say that, to me, the *sekha* is essentially *arahat*, and that, rigorously, I exclude him from *paṭiccasamuppāda anuloma*. Where *paṭiccasamuppāda* is concerned, we are dealing with the difference between the *puthujjana* and the *arahat*, and the question of the *sekha* simply *does not arise*. He is in between. The *sekha*, like the two-faced Roman god Janus (whose month this is), is looking both ways, to the past and to the future. The past is *anuloma*, and the future is *paṭiloma*, and if it is too late to include the *sekha* in *anuloma* it is too early to include him in *paṭiloma*. Or if you wish he is something of both.

2. There is no 'but' and 'when' about the *arahat*'s being *paṭiccasamuppāda paṭiloma*—he is *paṭiccasamuppāda paṭiloma* entirely, and in no way *anuloma*. *Anuloma* is *avijjāpaccayā*, and *paṭiloma* is *avijjānirodha*, and there is not the smallest trace of *avijjā* where the *arahat* is concerned. It is not possible to put 'him' back to *anuloma*, since, with cessation of *avijjā*, there is cessation of 'him' (*attavāda, asmimāna*)—*diṭṭh'eva dhamme saccato thetato Tathāgato anupalabbhamāne* (S. iv,384).[53] There is certainly no 'outside the *paṭiccasamuppāda* context' as far as persons are concerned, since *paṭiloma* is cessation of the person. Thus it is only if we think of the *arahat therī* Sonā as a *person*, as *somebody* (*sakkāya*), that she seems to be putting *herself* back to *anuloma* when she says: *pañcakkhandhā pariññātā tiṭṭhanti chinnamūlakā* (Therīgāthā 106).[54]

You suggest that when I describe the *arahat* I do so in terms other than negative to *pañc'upādānakkhandhā*; but when I describe him 'as such' I do not say he is *saupādāna*, any more than Sonā Therī when she describes herself 'as such'. But the fact is that no one, not even the Buddha, can describe an *arahat* in such a way as to be intelligible to a *puthujjana*; and the reason is, as you point out, that the whole of the *puthujjana*'s experience is *saupādāna*, including his experience of the *anupādāna arahat* (whether he sees him, thinks about him, visualizes or imagines him, or hears him described). Your account of the difficulties that you encounter when you consider the *arahat* and his robe, *as far as it goes*, is quite correct. (I say 'as far as it goes' since *to you* the *arahat*'s robe is to be worn '*by him*', whereas *to him* it is to-be-worn, not '*by me*' but '*on this body*'.)

For a *puthujjana* even the terms *khīṇāsava*, *akataññū*, and so on, *to the extent that they are intelligible to him*, are all *saupādāna*. In other words, it is impossible for a *puthujjana* to 'see' (= understand) an *arahat*—as soon as he does 'see' him he ceases to be a *puthujjana*. But this does not in the least mean that a *puthujjana* should not *try* to understand an *arahat*—he might succeed and then he would cease to be a *puthujjana*.

3. (i) *Āneñja* (*na iñjatī ti aneñjaṃ*), which literally means 'not shaking', seems to have two quite distinct connotations in the Suttas. In the first place it refers either (as in A. IV,190/ii,184) to the four *arūpa* attainments or more strictly (as in M. 106) to the fourth *jhāna* and *ākāsānañcāyatana* and *viññāṇañcāyatana*—note that the second and third *āneñjasappāya* refer to *both* these last two; and these are attainable by the *puthujjana*, the *sekha*, and the *arahat* alike, provided, of course, that they make the effort. See, for example, A. IV,172 (which should be a continuation of 171: ii,159), where certain *devā*, having been *nevasaññānāsaññāyatanūpagā* are liable to return to this world (which cannot happen to an *ariyasāvaka* in the same position). And see A. III,114/i,267 for the same of the first three of the *arūpa devā*. In the second place it refers to *arahattā*. *Anejo anupādāno sato bhikkhu paribbaje*[55] (Sn. 751). In both cases there is 'not shaking', but in two different senses. There is nothing mysterious about this; it is merely a question of Sutta usage.

(ii) As regards the passage you quoted from Majjhima 106/ii,264, I understand it in this way. When a *puthujjana* attains *nevasaññānāsaññāyatana* that is clearly enough *saupādāna*, that is, *sakkāya*. When a *sekha* attains this, he *sees* that it is *saupādāna*, that it is *sakkāya*. Now the condition for *upādāna* is *avijjā*, that is to say, *not seeing*—not seeing *upādāna* as *upādāna*. But the *sekha*, unlike the *puthujjana*, *does* see this, so his *upādāna* is *seen* and is also, therefore, *an-upādāna*. (As I have said before, all one can say of the *sekha* is *mā upādiyi*.) Similar remarks apply to the frequent passages in the Suttas where the *sekha* sees or considers or is urged to consider the *pañc'upādānakkhandhā* as *anicca* and so on. The *puthujjana* cannot see *pañc'upādānakkhandhā* as *anicca* or anything else, since he does not *see* them at all.

4. About *saḷāyatanā* and *phassa*. Within limits I follow your argument (except that I have no experience of the *dibbacakkhu* and cannot therefore usefully comment upon it), but I note that you seem to regard the *cakkhundriya* as 'subject'. The question remains, 'What do you mean by "subject"?'

In visual experience (considered alone) the eye does not appear (*na pātubhavati*) at all, either as *cakkhundriya* or as *maṃsacakkhu*, since vision itself is not visible, and the eye does not see itself. Since visual experience alone neither reveals *cakkhundriya* nor *maṃsacakkhu* there is (or should be) no justification for calling either of them *subject*. When other faculties (or a looking glass) are used the *maṃsacakkhu* appears (*pātubhavati*), but it appears as a phenomenon (to avoid using the word 'object' for the moment) amongst other phenomena, and, as such, has no claim to be called *subject*. In neither case is there any subject to be found. This being so, when these two experiences, visual and the other, occur together (as is usual), although there is the *constriction* you speak of (I would rather call it a *superposition*) there is no reason whatsoever for any 'discrepancy between subject and object'; for we have not found any subject. And in the *arahat* (do I disconcert you?) no discrepancy is, in fact, experienced, and no *dukkha*. It is only in the *puthujjana*, for whom an apparent *self* is manifest, and who necessarily divides things into *subject* and *object*, that the discrepancy you speak of can arise. But it seems to me that perhaps you do not find the approach by way of the *saḷāyatana* as congenial to you as the approach by way of *pañcakkhandhā*, and I shall not pursue the question any further.

5. In my early days in Ceylon I myself was something of a 'tidy-chart' maker, and I hoped and believed that it was possible to include all that the Suttas said in a single system—preferably portrayed diagrammatically on one very large sheet of paper. In those innocent days—which however did not last very long—I believed that the Commentaries knew what they were talking about. And I had the idea that everything that happened to me was *vipāka* and everything that I did about it (my reaction, that is, to the *vipāka*) was fresh *kamma*, which in turn produced fresh *vipāka*, and so on *ad inf*. And this is as tidy as anyone could wish.

Then I came across the Sutta that I transcribe below. This, as you will see, was enough to shatter my illusions, and it came as a bit of a shock (though also as a bit of a relief). In due course after asking people about it and getting no satisfactory explanation, I decided that my 'tidy idea' could be true only in a general sense, and that, in any case, it could not possibly be of any vital importance in the essential part of the Dhamma. Since then I have stopped thinking about it. Here is the Sutta (Vedanā Saṃy. 21/iv,229-31):[56]

Once the Auspicious One was staying near Rājagaha, at the Squirrel's feeding-ground in the Bamboo Grove.
Now at that time the Wanderer Sīvaka of the top knot approached the Auspicious One. Having approached, he exchanged courtesies and, having done so, sat down at one side. Sitting at one side the Wanderer Sīvaka of the top knot said this to the Auspicious One:
—There are some recluses and divines, Master Gotama, of such a belief, of such a view: 'Whatever this individual experiences, be it pleasant, unpleasant, or neutral, all that is due to former actions.' Herein what does Master Gotama say?
—Some feelings, Sīvaka, arise here (1) *with bile as their source*. That can be known by oneself, Sīvaka, how some feelings arise here with bile as their source; and that is reckoned by the world as truth, Sīvaka, how some feelings arise here with bile as their source. Therein, Sīvaka, the recluses and divines who are of such a belief, of such a view: 'Whatever this individual experiences, be it pleasant, unpleasant, or neutral, all that is due to former actions', they both go beyond what is known by themselves and go beyond what is reckoned as truth in the world. Therefore I say that these recluses and divines are in the wrong.
Some feelings, Sīvaka, arise here (2) *with phlegm as their source*...
Some feelings, Sīvaka, arise here (3) *with wind as their source*...
Some feelings, Sīvaka, arise here (4) *due to confluence of humours*...
Some feelings, Sīvaka, arise here (5) *born from seasonal change*...
Some feelings, Sīvaka, arise here (6) *born from improper care*...
Some feelings, Sīvaka, arise here (7) *due to exertion*...
Some feelings, Sīvaka, arise here (8) *born from the ripening of action*...
Therefore I say that these recluses and divines are in the wrong.

6. Let us return to §2. Your letter encourages me to think that, in a way, you understand your own failure to understand the *arahat*. And it is because I thought this also before that I felt it was worthwhile to speak of the 'sterility of making tidy charts'. The making of tidy charts (even if they are accurate, which is rarely the case—a chart of the Dhamma tends to distort it just as a map-maker distorts the curved surface that he represents on a flat sheet), the making of tidy charts, I say, is sterile because it is essentially *takka*, and the Dhamma is *atakkāvacara*. To make tidy charts, though not in itself reprehensible, does not lead to understanding. But it is useless to say such a thing to a convinced tidy-chart-maker—such as a commentator, who is satisfied that the Dhamma is understood when it is charted.

In your case, however, though you do tend to make tidy charts (it is an attitude of mind), there is also another aspect. You seem to be well aware that there is a discrepancy in your present position in that you are disconcerted when the *arahat* is described 'as such', and you are perhaps prepared to allow my statement that this is due to failure to see that things can be significant without being 'mine', that they can be teleological without being appropriated. And I think, also, that you are aware that *this*, in fact, is the central problem and that all else (including the tidy charts) is secondary and unimportant. This attitude is not sterile; and from the first it has been my principal concern, directly or indirectly, to encourage it and make it stand out decisively. As you have noted I have consistently underlined this matter (in whatever terms it has been stated) and rejected any possibility of arriving at a compromise solution. It is because you have been prepared to listen to this one thing that I have continued the correspondence. The other things we have discussed, except in so far as they have a bearing in this, are of little importance. But it is one thing for me to insist on this matter and quite another for you to see it. Even *bhikkhus* who heard the Dhamma from the Buddha's own mouth had sometimes to go away and work it out for themselves. *Tassa me Bhagavā ... so kho ahan ... paṭiladdho* (Bojjhaṅga Saṃy. 30/v,89-90).[57]

*Afternote*: You say that, as far as you see it, the *arahat*'s experience functions automatically. By this I presume that you mean it functions without any *self* or *agent* or *master* to direct it. But I do not say otherwise. All that I would add is that this automatically functioning experience has a complex teleological structure.

The *puthujjana*'s experience, however, is still more complex, since there is also *avijjā*, and there is thus appropriation as well as teleology. *But this, too, functions automatically, without any self or agent* to direct it. On account of the appropriation, however, it *appears* to be directed by a *self*, *agent*, or *master*. *Avijjā* functions automatically, but conceals this fact from itself. *Avijjā* is an automatically functioning blindness to its automatic functioning. Removal of the blindness removes the appropriation but not the teleology.

With best wishes,

Ñāṇavīra

**[SV. 13]** **15 January 1962**

Dear Bhante,

I received your previous letter most gratefully (today). I only want to acknowledge it herewith, because I would not be able to reply to it soon. [For the last two months I have been living utterly beyond my capacities—for a whole month I did not take my *dāna* (in its usual form)—and now I feel not well.] Apart from attending to your notes on *nāma-rūpa/viññāṇa*, I would have to make clear a certain outlook of mine, and so after having done so I earlier meant not to touch upon it—as if I could conceal anything from you—but now I will have to.

With deepest veneration,

V.

**[SV. 14]** **21 January 1962**

I feel that I owe a few lines to you, even though I am hardly able to give an adequate account of what happened; I am still rather benumbed.

Your notes on *viññāṇa nāmarūpa* have led me away from the abyss into which I have been staring for more than twelve years. (As if I did not know what I was asking from you! At the last moment you gave them to me, when I had almost abandoned all hope!) I had been addicted to a fallacious notion of the Teaching, which I held to be its clue, while, in reality, it was diametrically opposed to it. In accordance with my nature, however, I was given to it in such a way that, even though conscious that I was hanging between earth and sky, neither able to step forward nor backward, I could not surrender myself earlier than this, and, of course, after tremendous struggle. You must have seen what this notion consisted in, especially from my notes on *saññā*, though you did not directly name it, nor did I (or, rather, I somewhat concealed it)—I would have fallen if we had done so. Even now, *I* shall not do so, in order not to fall *from delusion into delusion*. It concerns the reality of things; I am not really interested in *kamma* and *vipāka*—those only served me to support my misconception, and well indeed! Even my latest argument on the *Arahat* consciously aimed at the same thing. I do not think you saw it—and that was good.

Your dispassionate description of *nāmarūpa* and *viññāṇa* has made me realize that I was unable to remove the tint of passion from things—while at the same time denying their existence,[a] I do not know how I stood that position for such a long time. I do not know either by what miraculous skill you have guided me to a safe place where at last I can breathe freely. It should scarcely be necessary to say that the question of *pañcakkhandhā* was not just one among others, but was *the* question. Your interpretation of *cetanā* as intention *and* significance, which to me were just the *antipodes*, was such a nuisance that only your last letter compelled me to enter into the matter at all; I had so far just pushed it aside. The connection *cetanā–saṅkhāra* had entirely escaped my consciousness; but once I had made up my mind to follow it up, I recovered from my own notes *sabbe sattā saṅkhāra-ṭṭhitikā cha sañcetanā-kāyā* = *saṅkhārakkhandha*[58]. I had never any difficulty to follow your argument

a. Or more concisely, *because* of doing so.

'*omnis determinatio...*', provided, of course, I took it as pertaining to *saṅkhārā*, and not to *cetanā*.[a] I can see things clearly now, though not, of course, all its implications. In that way, the subject is removed from experience, and the *pañcakkhandhā* can function apart from *upādāna*. Thus the question is settled. I have lost a dimension of thought, at least to the degree to grasp this matter, i.e. my own *upādāna*.

The whole thing has a complicated history. Unlike you, I did not primarily gain access to the Teaching by studying the Suttas on my own. I was under the influence of a powerful individual for six years, until I came to Ceylon. He unduly stressed certain aspects of the Teaching, which had a fatal affect on me on account of my being by nature inclined to an 'idealistic' outlook. And, also, my German translations (Karl Eugen Neumann), that I imbibed to an extreme degree, did the same. As I told you, I am not independent. I shiver when I think of the delusion I was shrouded in. How difficult it is to follow the Buddha!

You have seen that I took your repeated references to the *puthujjana* in connection with me as a challenge—though I once denied it proudly. In your last letter you have put that challenge masterly; I could not possibly not take it up—and this time seriously, no less seriously indeed than the other matter. In fact, I was always passing from one thing to the other—through the depths of my being. (In connection with this, I have to confess something that will hardly come out from my pen. I must, however, at once say that, while doing it, I denied only myself—not you; there was no disrespect in doing it towards you. I had recognized your letter as precious, so I have written already, but, nevertheless, the next day, at night, I burnt it—along with all the rest. Even your precious notes! [That appeared, however, quite different at that moment—a temptation of Māra, who seemed to whisper that were teleological experience, without a self, and free from all *dukkha*, could be a fine thing as such!] I cannot even ask your pardon, for I did not offend you. I was constantly trying to find my own image in you by reading the letters; you know that I am passionate, and, accordingly I acted, that is all. And I got the results soon as I had done it. So the highest purpose of all your *hitānukampa* has been achieved, and, moreover, I have a good memory, and know almost every word that you have written.) All that I can say now as regards the *puthujjana* is this. I can only put it as a

a. I found that - was 'I'!

question, for I do really not know what happened in 1949; I was too inexperienced *and had never touched a text* when the Dhamma almost forced itself upon me and brought about great, and lasting, changes in my life. Can the *puthujjana* really make such a quest as mine has been, even though, as yet, negatively, his own, so as never even for a second to depart from it, as, in fact, I did? Whatever it may be, I am no longer worried about it, now that I have got rid of a great deal of delusion. I did at least never touch upon the *Arahat*, though you seem to blame me for it. I am perhaps really a religious person—the *Arahat* was sacred to me, in the sense of being taboo; and it is only now that I appear to have been permitted into his presence. Such an attitude, too, I do not know whether the *puthujjana* is capable of. But I am *asking* you, only that. Finally, did I not consistently adhere to *you*, ever since 'Proof of Rebirth'? You do not know, of course, that you had always been guiding me, even though I did not take heart to approach you. Even now, I have each time to make up my mind to write you, for everything that I say appears to me so principally inappropriate that really I would prefer not to say anything—if only could afford to. I reached out for you in order to lift myself to your heights, and in that I found the only justification for doing so—and, of course, you have granted it.

In deepest veneration,

V.

N.B. By the way, I duly received back my notes on the *Ariyasāvaka*. Thank you very much for your comments.

## Anulomikā khanti?[59]

**[SV. 15]** **23 January 1962**

Dear Bhante,

That I burnt your letters and notes was the most dangerous act that I ever committed. I did it as a *puthujjana*. I was indeed *bāhira*; I had no grain of *saddhā*; I did not know what *saddhā* is. I realize now, where I most urgently need them, that I cannot remember the most essential parts, for the simple reason that those were the most obscure to me. I know that you will forgive me; it is hardly possible to offend you, though I am fully conscious that you gave your innermost to me. From the following you will see that I am also worth to be forgiven.

Yesterday, when I once more tried to see *pañcakkhandhā* guided by your notes, I suddenly came across the thorn that had been stinking me uninterruptedly since 1949. And I discovered—*dukkha*. The conceit on which I had built my *Ariyasāvakahood* was this thorn, which, somehow, I had received along with the 'Dhanmma'. But I know now that the *puthujjana* can take upon himself any *dukkha*—even for the 'Dhamma'—because he does not know anything else. My conceit, however, did not stand out decisively (I hardly ever thought about it, except during certain periods, where circumstances were very trying) until now; and the moment I realized what it really *means* to be *puthujjana*, I ceased to be one.

sticking

this claim can be accepted

I do still not know clearly what happened to me in 1949.[a] I shall, therefore, not tell anything much about it. As I have repeatedly indicated, the matter was bound up with an individual (a well-known Buddhist lecturer in Hamburg; not Dr. Hecker; we are both pupils of him.) After I had that glimpse of insight mentioned above I fell into an emotional state—I do so by turns—as regards that individual[60]. He has great control over many, he is a mystical man, and he has made us feel that he is an *Ariyasāvaka*. I firmly believed it, until last evening. Calling to mind what had happened between us, as well as his whole life, I almost committed

P.D. presumably[1]

---

**a.** It has to do with religion and eros, as I discovered after my latest insight. And I had at that time a vision that I remember dimly had to do with rebirth. Nevertheless—I came from mathematics; and my first scheme of the 'Dhamma' was indeed a mathematical formula! With my birth and very early childhood are connected certain mystical and obscure occurrences. I grew up with foster parents.

a great offence in 'dethroning' him along with myself. It was hard to see through it. I may say that he is as much of an approximation to the *puthujjana* as you are to the *Arahat*, but he is[a] not a *puthujjana*. I seem to be confronted with the most discrepant phenomena; my whole life was that I mention this thing to you, because it was of such an importance to me. I won a victory over myself; and when I awoke this morning I had found refuge in the Dhamma, and I realized everything (or a great many things) that we had been discussing. At least, Bhante, I did not conceal myself; I was proud, conceited, and, most of all, deluded, but I was straight. My strongest weapon was humility—though I can see now also how you look upon it; *anatimānī*[61] is somewhat different; only an *Ariyasāvaka* possesses it, I think. I fought a fight knowing not for what—and you have helped me most wonderfully.

I begin now to discover the Dhamma. I can just stay in one place and see everything passing before my eyes that I knew without knowing. It is an entirely new landscape. I had concerned myself much with the most essential problems—and yet the meaning was hidden from me. I found another diagram on *nāmarūpa-viññāṇa* that I had made years ago. I never looked at it—but it was myself, wholly. Like my argument on the *Arahat*, it was quite correct, so far as it goes; the only thing that was wrong about it was that is was these[62]. I think most of these ideas I took down after your 'Proof of Rebirth'. Even those days you were a challenge to me. I do not know, but perhaps you do, *why* your notes on *viññāṇa* etc. are opening out what I could not find in the texts. I mistook it all. What your notes essentially reveal to me is to allow things to be (present), whilst the Suttas seemed to say that I must deny them. Once I had found justification of *cetanā* = *saṅkhārā* (as already indicated), I laid hold of your notes in the way that I do things—either-or. I wrestled with them to the utmost, always in turns with emotional states. Today I arrived at *viññāṇa*. I saw, though at the moment it appears somewhat dim, the difference *viññāṇa—bhava*: the self that I meant was to be denied in the *pañcakkhandhā*, I did not find, because I did not know anything at all about them. I find that my position was most curious (but, of course, there is nothing particular in it, as I[b] now understand)

---

**a.** Probably (after my latest insight).

**b.** I could express this more clearly; but not while writing the letter, which serves a more general purpose.

—I had no time to investigate into the nature of the *pañcakkhandhā*, because, radically, I negated everything as soon as I became aware of it. My blindness really was total. I brought myself into immense tension, and, in fact, it is strain that I also now experience to an extreme degree, especially while writing this (but I feel that I should do so). I can also understand something about *akālika* now. I had no idea that things can stand in relation to each other other than temporally (do I use the word now correctly? I think so.) I meant it was a most sublime idea that *rūpa* should be *saññā*; it is crude indeed. I discovered the real meaning of *anicca* in connection with *viññāṇa*, and many other things.

advance notice

It is hard for me to imagine that you do not know everything already, but, remembering that you are not a visionary (unnecessary to say that I know you are indefinitely much more), I must give you at least some evidence now itself, for I do really not know what will happen the next moment (I may not be able to keep full control over myself—as I appear to others). I would like you to send me some more notes, especially about *viññāṇa*; I did not quite get the latter part of your para. I and II.

In deepest veneration,

V.

*Sammattaniyāmaṃ okkanti?* [63]

**[SV. 16]** **undated**

Dear Bhante,

This night, after I had written the letter to you, *at last*—I saw the Buddha!

In deepest veneration,

V.

see next letter

N.B. There came a gale along with it—I think it was you, indicating also this to me.

V.

*Sotāpattiphala*, probably

**[SV. 17]** **25 January 1962**

Dear Bhante,

? The wind-element has told me everything that went on last night. Now the veil (the most disconcerting) has been removed from your face, and I can see you quite clearly. Now I know that *Nibbāna* is real—I did really not know that an *Arahat* was hidden among the *tayo puggalā*, and ? you carefully have avoided commenting on this point in my note on the *Ariyasāvaka*, though I had put a big red mark there. I thought '*Arahā vā*' was a misreading in my Sinhala text. I could never understand the Sunakkhatta Sutta[64], but now I can. I began to discover the matter last evening. Now I also can understand the *Paññāvimutta Arahat*, and the difference *cetovimutti–paññāvimutti*—also on that you made no remark at all. I know that there was a Sutta stating an *indriya-vematta*, but, of course, I understood nothing of the matter.

Do you think anyone ever understood you? A *man* could never have done so; but now many will have a better chance. I told you, everything was one riddle in you. I have seen the Buddha as *Paṭiccasamuppāda*, and *Yo paṭiccasamuppādaṃ passati so* I heard the Mūlapariyāya Sutta intoned—but I was tossing about in pains seeing it as *saṅkhārā*. I could never have found *Nibbāna*—with your face veiled. This you must have felt. I began to see the *Paññāvimutta* *who said?* *Arahat* in you before you had attained it—seeing at the same time that there was no *āsava* in a *Paññāvimutta Arahat*. O, I do not know yet, but this thing was certainly not only *my* last formula. Everything was evident in our discussion—even the question of *upadhi*—which was evidently! probably the only thing that I had rightly grasped. It will still take me time to relax; I am simply passing from one emotional state into the other—but now, at last, I have found you.

The Dvāyatanapassana Sutta did certainly occupy a prominent place in your thoughts, did it not? It was my most favourable Sutta. The double hierarchy that you spoke of was a tremendous thing; it was ? self-destructive, just as my diagram of *nāma-rūpa-viññāṇa*; no other individual could have stood it; it was tension in itself. There had to come only one new phenomena into it—and that was I. In a way, the foolish ripple shook the rock.

Do you know that the wind-element obeys you? It is to me the sweetest comfort. This also I knew; it is your most sublime *anāpānasati* that surrenders it. You need not write to me, (or of course, as you please).

I could tell you many more things, but it is not so important.

In deepest veneration,

V.

*Letting off steam.*

**[L. 150]** **29 January 1962**

Dear Sister,[66]

Thank you for your letter of the 25th. You have, I fear, returned to your habit of writing in riddles, which makes it extremely difficult for a person like me to follow you. I do not see why an *arahat* should be hidden amongst the *kāyasakkhi*, *diṭṭhipatto*, and *saddhāvimutto*—all these three have something further to do, as you may see from the Kītāgiri Sutta (M. 70), and this cannot be said of any *arahat*. I did not comment on this since I agreed that the reading '*arahī vā*' (which is not in the P.T.S. edition, even as a v.l.) was wrong. I still think it is.

It may seem to you that the wind-element obeys me, but to me it appears otherwise. The wind element comes and *lodges* in my intestines for a large part of each day and causes a persistent discomfort that nearly prevents me from doing any *ānāpānasati* at all. This has been going on for the last ten years, and at present seems to be getting worse (it is largely for this reason that I have spent so much time thinking about the Dhamma rather then practising *jhāna*, which was my prime reason for coming to Ceylon; but things having turned out in the way they have, I can have no reason for complaint). As a means of communication I prefer the post to the wind-element—though it is no doubt slower it is less liable to deliver a corrupt text. It may be that you have seen in me the *arahat* or that the wind-element has told you that I actually am *arahat*; but the plain fact is that I am not *arahat* and, partly on account of obstruction by the wind-element, I have no great hopes of becoming one in this lifetime. I am a long way from *arahattā*, I have far to go before reaching that. What exactly I am is a matter of no great importance, and for reasons of Vinaya, which have to be complied with, discussion of this matter is not advisable. It is obvious enough that you, with your present understanding, may arrive at certain general conclusions about what I am or am not; but that is neither here no there. In any case I must ask you, as far as possible, to keep these conclusions to yourself—it will be a considerable embarrassment to me to be talked about, and it will not serve any useful purpose.

You ask if I think that anyone ever understood me. As far as one person may understand another I have both understood, and been understood by, other people. But there are always limitations in this; however long one has known another person he can still behave in unexpected ways. No person, in the normal way, ever *completely* understands another. There are certain things about me that have been better understood by men and certain things that have been better understood by women, but nobody has ever completely understood me. At present it is a matter of complete indifference to me whether anybody understands me, or thinks he understands me,—*as an individual*, that is to say. On the other hand, it is possible that a certain person may understand and see the *Buddha's* Teaching, and it may happen that another person may come to see this Teaching from this first person; but when this happens it cannot properly be said that the second person *understands the first person* in the sense discussed above—what can properly be said is that both understand the Teaching. And anyone else who understands the Teaching (no mattter by what means) comes to join the first two; they all understand one another in so far as they all understand the same thing; but as far as understanding one another as individuals goes, they may be complete strangers. No doubt you will follow this. If so, I would ask you not to confuse the two things. To me, you, as an individual, are nearly a stranger; I am not interested in you *as an individual* except in so far as it is necessary for the purpose of communicating the Dhamma. When this has been done (and, as far as I can judge, it *has* been done), you become of interest to me *as one who understands the Dhamma*, but not otherwise. Conversely, I very much doubt whether you understand very much about me *as an individual*, however it may be in the other sense. I am aware, bacause you have told me, that you are an emotional person and that you depend much upon personal relationships with others. Knowing this fact, I made use of it in our recent correspondence—communication of the Dhamma was made on a personal basis (you would never have accepted it on an intellectual basis); and the bonfire of my letters was the logical conclusion (though I did not actually anticipate this). You have built up a certain picture me, a certain idea of me, *as an individual* (to you, as *puthujjana*, I represented the *arahat*), and since this was necessary to you I did not interfere with it. But now that it is no longer necessary to you (if you have seen the Dhamma you are quite independent of anyone else), I take the liberty of saying that there is no reason whatsoever for supposing that your idea of me has any essential connexion with what I am in reality. I lay some emphasis on this matter since you seem to suggest in your letter that it is necessary to understand me as an individual in order to understand the Dhamma (you say that now many will have a better chance of understanding me; which almost sounds as if you propose to set about *interpreting* me to other people—is this what you mean?). [In this connexion I find your reference to the double hierarchy as 'tension in itself' most obscure. And in what way does the entry of the new phenomenon—yourself—affect it? The double hierarchy as a picture of the fundamental structure of negatives and as an instrument of thought was valid and remains valid—indeed it enables me to give myself a more precise idea of the nature of the fundamental appropriation of things (when there is *avijjā*) then any that I have actually set down on paper. It is one of the things that has not been self-destructive).]

It may seem to you, perhaps, that I am being unnecessarily hard on you, especially at the present moment with your newly won *dhammapīti*. In my last letter I told you that I was delighted; and it remains true. I *am* delighted at your success—you have won a great victory over yourself, a victory that cannot be taken away. (I am a very cautious person, and I keep saying to myself 'I *hope* there is no mistake, I *hope* she really does see'. But from [? illeg.] your letter I *think* there is no mistake). But I must say also this: that if you want to make progress (and progress has to be made), you cannot afford to indulge in emotional states. I said that you are rapidly becoming a tower of strength; but it will not be 'rapidly' without a good deal of *nekkhammasaṅkappa*. Do you not see the *dukkha* of emotions? Why torment yourself with myths of your own creation? Practise *samatha*, and let the myths die of neglect.

With best wishes,

Ñāṇavīra

**[SV. 18]** **5 February 1962**

Venerable Ñāṇavīra Thero
Dear Bhikkhu

I have to tell you something very sad. Sister Vajira has gone off her head. Please do not answer any of her letters on the dhamma. Some girls have stayed with her for the last few days & came & told Mrs. Nimalasuriya that she is very bad—we are trying to bring her to Colombo. I am on my way to Mrs. Weerasuria to discuss & and make arrangements about Sister Vajira—Dr. & Mrs. Nimalasuriya may go to bring her—This is a hurried note to inform you as she may write some nonsense to you.

Hope you are keeping well.

With Metta,

Dayika (M. Salgado)

**[SV. 19]** **12 February 1962**

Venerable Ñāṇavīra Thero
Dear Bhikkhu

Thanks for your letter of the 7th. We went on the 6th & brought Sister to Colombo. She ran away in the night & was walking along the streets, several followed her & with great difficulty put her into a car. Dr. Nimalasuriya, Dr. Shelton Fernando & their wifes along with me forced her into a car & and took her to Sulamin Hospital at 2 a.m. She is under Dr. Tudor's treatment. This is a private hospital at Borella. Now she is much better after the treatment; there also, twice she had jumped through the window & roamed about, but the nurse & attendants managed to bring her back. Now Sister Vajira says she wants to get into a saree & at times she says she wants to go to Germany.

We are wondering what to do with her. By this same post I am writing to Rev. Nyanaponika also.

I hope you are keeping well. Rev. Sir you also should not allow yourself to be weak. Kindly let me know what you require? Do you want "Sanatogen" I can get Hinton to supply your needs do please write & let me know. Do you take B.G. Phos?

With Metta,

Dayika M. Salgado

**[SV. 20]** **14 February 1962**

V. has recovered. Is very anxious to return home. My condition is not worse. Hope to return to the island in March.

With Vandanā

Siridhamma

**[SV. 21]** **24 February 1962**

Dear Ven. Sir,

Mrs. Saldago informs me that Sister Vajira left yesterday. All her requirements had been attended to. They had supplied her with clothes to the value of two to three hundred rupees.

Although she was speaking of marriage at one stage, prior to her departure, she had said that she would go back to her foster-parents and lead a quiet life (single). According to Dr. Nim. she was not normal when she left. Had she been normal, she would not have failed to return the Majjhima translations to the hermitage and a Pali dictionary I had lent her. Mrs. Salgado said she would get them for me.

I my leave for the hermitage on the 3rd. Trust you are keeping well.

With Vandanā

Siridhamma

**[SV. 22]** **26 February 1962**

Venerable Ñāṇavīra Thero
Dear Bhikkhu

Just a line to inform you that Sister Vajira left for Germany on the 22nd. She had recovered but not perfectly normal. She was well enough to go by herself, without anyone else to look after her. The German Embassy made arrangements for her trip. Since she entered Hospital on the 7th Feb she gave up her nun's life & became a lay woman. She said she does not want to be a nun again so we made arrangements for her to go much against her wish. Since she gave up robes & not perfectly normal there was no one to support her. Rev. Narada & Rev. Nyanaponika both wanted her to go & also the Embassy people did not want her to stay here.

Anyway we gave her the best of comforts till she took the plane right from Sulaman Hospital.

Hope you are keeping well. If there is anything you require kindly let me know.

Dayika
M. Salgado
Mrs. M.S. Salgado

Exit unwanted *ariyasāvikā*

# AFTERWORD

**[L. 100/107]** **24 August 1964**

Dear Mr. Samaratunga,

It is interesting to read your reactions to the letters I sent you. Sister Vajirā is an extremely passionate and self-willed person, with strong emotions, and, apparently, something of a visionary. In other words, she is totally different, temperamentally, from either of us (though in different ways). Besides, she is a woman. You will see, in her letters, how she alternates between moods—one could almost say *attacks*—of emotional periods and of admirable clear-headedness. During the former her letters tend to become incoherent, and she *assumes* that her reader is in a similar state and can fill in all the gaps. But, quite clearly, she is perfectly *at home* in her emotions, in a way that you and I find difficult to understand: emotion, for her, is quite normal, as it is for nearly all women. And it must not be forgotten that she was living more or less alone with her thoughts, and solitude always has the effect of magnifying and intensifying one's inner life. I do not at all think that Sister Vajirā's emotional manifestations are (or were—since they are now past history) anything to be alarmed at, and far less a sign of mental disorder. Certainly, she does not find them alarming, and even gives due notice to other people in case *they* do.

One thing must be kept in mind when reading her letters: for about a dozen years she had had the idea that the Buddha taught that *nothing really exists*, and she had been developing this mistaken notion in solitude. But, being a mistake, it leads nowhere except to a state of exasperation and nervous tension (there is someone else, known to both of us, who is doing the same thing, and he is certainly not achieving inward calm). Furthermore, she was convinced (her teacher was evidently partly responsible) that she had already reached the first *magga* (though not the *phala*); and this was the cause of her impatience, bad temper, and extreme conceit.[a] I was quite aware of her discourteous attitude and even bad manners, but I said nothing at that time since I did not want to prejudice the outcome of our correspondence by pulling her up over a matter of secondary importance. We Europeans are much more accustomed to casual manners, and (perhaps wrongly) stand less on our dignity in this matter than Easterners. (The act of *vandanā*, for me, still keeps a faint air of artificiality—we are not brought up with it.) And now, as I think, there is no longer any need to check her.

About the burning of my letters, I rather think that you must have misread what she says. You quote a passage that you (quite rightly) describe as a 'song of victory',[b] but then go on to say that this idea was completely changed for you by the incident of the burning of the letters. From this I gather that you take the burning of the letters to have taken place *after* her would-be 'victory'. But I think this is a mistake. She herself says that it was *after* she had burnt my letters that she 'got the result'. The letter in question gives the result first (it was, after all, the important thing) and then goes on to apologize for having burnt the letters in a fit of passion.

Nothing is done in this world, either good or bad, without passion. 'Mental stability' too often means lack of passion. But passion must be disciplined and used intelligently and some people need a teacher to do this for them. 'By means of craving, craving must be abandoned' say the Suttas (A.IV,159/ii,445-46). That, in any case, was how I read it. She had (so I gathered) been wrestling with the meaning of my letters and getting nowhere, until finally, in a fit of exasperation, she had decided that they were all wrong and had consigned them (and me too, by implication) to the flames. It was only then that she grasped the meaning of what I had written—hence her later remorse. From her point of view it was indeed a 'dangerous act' since she had not yet understood them when she destroyed them. But (I am inclined to think) some such act

a. This explains, for example, the letter beginning 'Dear Bhikkhu'—it is quite evident that she knows better, since all her later letters (I think this was an early one) are perfectly respectful. And the Ven. Kassapa Thera once complained that she had come into his room and taken a chair without so much as 'By your leave.'

b. I am unable to see that it could have been written by a *puthujjana*, even if he were trying to deceive. It would never occur to him to add the part about 'losing a dimension of thought'. One must actually have had the experience to know how exactly this describes it.

of despair was perhaps necessary to release an accumulation of tension before the meaning of the letters could occur to her. Attainment does not come at the moment when we are making a conscious effort to attain, because at that time we have *uddhacca-kukkucca*, 'distraction and worry', but rather at the unexpected moment when we relax after an apparently fruitless effort.

For my part I am satisfied (judging solely from the letters) that, however strange her behaviour may have seemed to her well-wishers in Colombo, there was nothing in it to contradict my opinion. What you speak of as the 'breaking point' was (as I see it) no more than the entry into a particularly strong (and pleasurable) emotional state consequent upon the realization (which, at the beginning especially, can be breathtaking) that 'nothing matters any more'. I don't suppose she was within a hundred miles of telling the people who were caring for her what the reason was for her condition. Certainly, her last letter, for all its emotional colouring, gives no suggestion that she is in any way unhappy or distressed, or even that she has any doubts about her new state. And you will observe that I am quietly but firmly dismissed at the end of the letter. Whatever else happened, one thing is certain—she no longer finds herself in any way dependent upon me. A psychoanalyst, at least, would be gratified with that result!

About *paṭiccasamuppāda*. I do not see that it is possible for anyone to reconcile my view of *paṭiccasamuppāda* with the three-life view. If anyone says that they are both correct, then I would suggest that he has failed to understand what I have written—though, as I freely admit, that may be because I have failed to make myself clear. As to Sister Vajirā's statements, I think you will find that one was written 'before' and one 'after'. This distinction, actually, is crucial; and Sister Vajirā's change of view is significant.

P.S. The word 'sister' (*bhaginī*) seems to be used in the Suttas as a quite general term or form of address for women, particularly by *bhikkhus*. In my letters to her I addressed Sister Vajirā as 'Dear Upāsikā'. I do not see that there is any objection to the word 'sister' as used for *dasasil upāsikā*. Laymen used to address *bhikkhunīs* as *ayye*, which means 'lady', but an *upāsikā* is not a *bhikkhunī*. In the Suttas, *bhikkhus* used to address *bhikkhunīs* as *bhaginī*.

**[L. 101/108, *fragment*] 30 August 1964**

[...] Amongst people of Buddhist countries it is, I think, not properly understood (quite naturally) that, generally speaking, Europeans who become Buddhists belong necessarily to the 'unstable-minded' and not to the 'stable-minded'. The Buddha's Teaching is quite alien to the European tradition, and a European who adopts it is a rebel. A 'stable-minded' European is a Christian (or at least he accepts the Christian tradition: *religion* for him—whether he accepts it or not—, *means* Christianity; and a *Buddhist* European is not even 'religious'—he is simply a lunatic).

But in a Buddhist country, naturally, to be a Buddhist is to be 'stable-minded', since one is, as it were, 'born a Buddhist'. And 'born-Buddhists' find it difficult to understand the unstable-minded European Buddhist, who treats the Buddha's Teaching as a wonderful new discovery and then proposes, seriously, to practise it.[a] The stable-minded traditional Buddhist cannot make out what the unstable-minded European Buddhist is making such a fuss about.[b] [...]

---

**a.** It often happens, of course, that he has got it upside-down and inside-out; but at least he has enthusiasm (at any rate to begin with).

**b.** And so it is not in the least astonishing that Sister Vajirā's supporters are scandalized when she 'goes off her head' for a fortnight with joy (which is my view of what happened).

**[L. 102/109]** **31 August 1964**

As to that Sutta you mention (A. IV,159/ii,144-7): a *bhikkhunī* sends for the Ven. Ānanda Thera, being infatuated with him and hoping perhaps for sexual intercourse. The Ven. Ānanda understands the situation and gives her a suitable Dhamma-talk. He tells her (i) that this body is a product of food and that, depending on food, food is to be given up (a *bhikkhu*'s body is made of food, but he must go on taking food to keep alive and practise the Dhamma if he wishes to give up food in the future by not being reborn); (ii) that this body is a product of craving and that, depending on craving, craving is to be given up (a *bhikkhu*, having been born on account of craving in his previous life, hears that so-and-so has become an *arahat* and, craving that for himself, sets to work to get it; and in course of time he succeeds, his success being, precisely, the giving up of all craving); (iii) the same with *māna* or conceit (the *bhikkhu*, hearing that so-and-so has become an *arahat*, thinks 'I'm as good as he is, and if he can do it, so can I', and sets to work; and in due course, prompted by conceit, he puts an end to conceit); (iv) that this body is a product of copulation, and that the Buddha has said that (for monks) copulation is absolutely not to be practised. In (ii), the *bhikkhu craves for arahatship* since he thinks in terms of 'I' or 'self' ('When shall I attain that?'), and all such thoughts contain *bhavataṇhā*, though of course here there is no *sensual* craving (*kāmataṇhā*). But anyone who thinks 'When shall *I* become an *arahat*?' is *ipso facto* failing to understand what it means to be an *arahat* (since being an *arahat* means *not* thinking in terms of 'I'). So, on account of his craving for *arahat*ship, he sets out to get it. But, since he does not understand what *arahat*ship is, he does not know what it is that he is seeking; and when, in due course, he *does* come to know what it is he is seeking, he has *ipso facto* found it (or at least the first installment of it). It is by making use of *bhavataṇhā* that he gives up *bhavataṇhā* (and *a fortiori* all other kinds of *taṇhā*). I think that Sister Vajirā, in her last letter but one, says that she had not known what it was that she had been fighting against, but that she now saw that the solution had been staring her in the face all the time without her being able to see it. This describes the situation very well. It is *because* of *bhavataṇhā* that, *with the Buddha's help*, we make an attempt to recognize *bhavataṇhā* and succeed in doing so, thereby bringing *bhavataṇhā* to an end.

I fully agree with you that the curtain came down on the drama too suddenly. I was hoping for a further letter but was disappointed. And when she was packed off there was no further chance of meeting her and filling in the gaps. But if in fact she really did cease to be a *puthujjana* (and I see no reason to doubt it), then we are perhaps fortunate in having as much as we do have in the way of a written record of an actual attainment of the *magga* (and probably also of the *phala*) as it took place. An account written afterwards from memory would not have the dramatic force of these letters which are so striking.

HAMBURG, 14.10.1928 – MASCHEN, 7.12.1991

# BIOGRAPHY OF HANNELORE WOLF (SISTER VAJIRĀ)

*Hellmuth Hecker*[67]

In an upper class neighbourhood in Hamburg a wife lived in well to do conditions. She had two sons and no concerns. However, somehow she sought for a deeper meaning and came across Schopenhauer while reading. Then in 1927 a wandering preacher of a Christian sect appeared in Hamburg who appealed to her religious feelings and she followed him. Soon she got a child from him: Hannelore Wolf. Although the sect worshipped the child as the God-sent heir to the master, he himself abandoned mother and child without giving any financial support. They had to live in St. Pauli in a damp cellar. The government child inspector, on the reason of neglect, gave the child to foster parents. Her foster father Bading was an employee at the department of finances in Hamburg. Hannelore grew up in this family together with two adopted sisters. After finishing school she followed a course in technical design. In the meantime, her physical father had turned to politics and had ended up in a mental home before the war. Her physical mother suffered a similar fate and died in the early 1950's.

Hannelore was looking for religious meanings. In early summer 1949 she noticed a poster that announced a four part introductory course to the teachings of the Buddha. It was held by Paul Debes. Thus she went to the university's main lecture theatre where the talks were given on 23.vi.1949. After the first talk she hesitated to go again, but nevertheless did so. The talk was especially agreeable to her. I wrote to my friend Fritz Schäfer in Itzehoe on 25.vi.1949:

> 'It was great. It was dead silent in the hall and nobody left (same as during talk No. 1). The spiritual contact was remarkably close. Although nothing new was really said, I was completely taken.'

Hannelore was so much impressed that she listened to the next talks, came to the seminary group of Debes, and took part in his first 'weeks of investigation' in an Adults' Education College in the Lüneburger Heide area on 6-27 August 1949. I noticed her there. On her belt she wore a medallion with the inscription *'In tempestate securitas'*. She told me that the summary of the Buddha's teaching was: 'To increase good, decrease evil, avoid staying on.' The next year she only participated during three days of the three weeks study course of the second 'weeks of investigation'. There she said that she wanted to become a nun in Ceylon. She remarked: 'All of you like it too much around here.'

During both courses of 'weeks of investigation' she had become friendly with Mrs. Erika von der Osten (PhD). [...] She suggested to Hannelore to become a private teacher for her son and daughter. Thus Hannelore moved to their place in September 1950, and lived quite happily with the family. When Mrs. von der Osten's husband returned from internment as a prisoner of war, the family moved back to Hannover. Hannelore returned to Hamburg and worked as a technical designer again. She also joined the circle of Debes-friends there.

She wrote to me in London on 12 April 1953, where I did some studies in order to prepare legislative on Army Service Refusal:

> 'All of you are lovely and terribly worldly people. Always hanging out in the world without ever finding satisfaction.'

After returning from London, I met her frequently at Dhamma talks. In autumn 1953 she founded, together with two female friends from the Debes group and me, a Dhamma discussion group [...] Hannelore played an influential role in the Buddhist circles and tried to deflate tensions.

In June 1954 the Sinhalese monk Ven. Nārada suddenly turned up in Hamburg. Hannelore took the opportunity trying to get a chance to go to Ceylon as a nun. Debes had tried in vain to find such an opportunity through sister Upalavannā. At the instigations of Ven. Nārada 'Hamburg Buddha Mandala' was founded, out of which the Buddhist Society of Hamburg evolved on 9 October 1954. Ven. Nārada gave Pali names to many Buddhists and Hannelore, called Hanna, became Vajirā. The founding of the society and Hanna's ambitions caused a lot of unrest. My brother in law, Wolfgang Seel, also a Buddhist and later working as a psychologist, who had good character knowledge, was of the opinion that it was much too early for Hanna to go to Ceylon and to isolate herself completely from her cultural background. It would not be good for her.

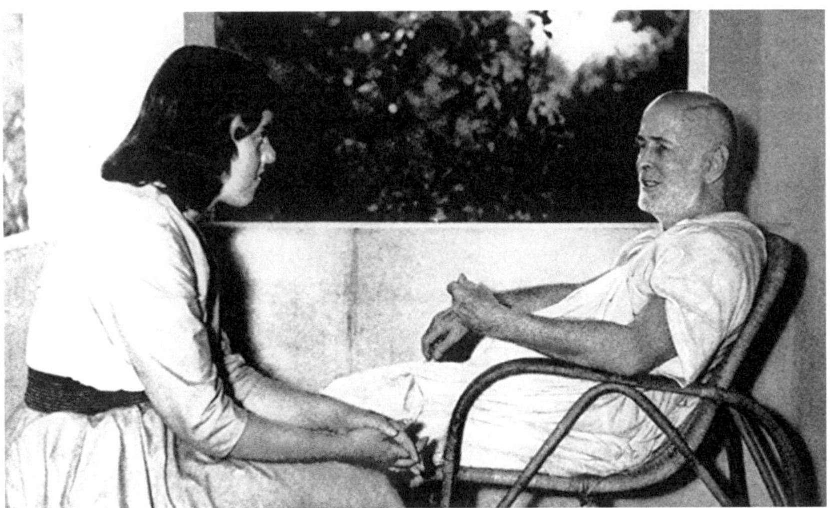

The Ven. Nyānatiloka talking in Spring 1955 to Hannelore Wolf (later Sister Vajirā) who arrived in Ceylon from Hamburg. (Photograph: Dr. Winfried Petri, Schliersee)

After much turmoil she finally got a chance to go to Ceylon. In 1955 the Vihāra Mahādevi Hermitage at Biyagāma near Colombo was to be opened, where Buddhist nuns (*Dasa-sīl-upāsikā* = ten precept female followers) lived. Through the mediation of Ven. Nārada and Mrs. Salgado, the leader of a Buddhist women society supporting the Sangha, she could go there. After I had vouched for any possible costs of a return journey, she got her visa and departed on 1 April 1955 from Genoa by the ship called 'Asia'. I brought her on board and she said:

> 'Now I go away to meet the real life, and you return, hopefully in order to get fed up with the world.'

On board she got to know the astronomer Dr. Winfried Petri, who later converted to Buddhism. He was on his way to Ceylon to watch a solar eclipse. Together with him she visited Ven. Nyānatiloka and Ven. Nyānaponika in Kandy as well as the Island Hermitage of Polgasduwa, about which she wrote:

> 'After I had seen this island, I can only say: If someone does not become a saint here, he will never become one, because he is not internally capable of doing so, as the external conditions are perfect.

> ... On the whole island there are only three monks and an *upāsaka*. Solitude is difficult to bear.'

Sister Vajirā as a buddhist nun, 1955(?), source: Helmuth Hecker.

After she had moved from the house of Mrs. Salgado to Biyagāma on 6 May 1955 where at that time ten young Singhalese women lived as nuns, she also took on the 10 rules and was ordained as Sister Vajirā by Ven. Nārada on the full moon of July. About her life she wrote:

> 'By the way, I live here as if in a fairy-tale. In my whole life I have not had it so good and beautiful as here... I can't describe the peace entering my heart when I see a sunset, which is different every day... I am surprised how gentle I have become, in any case, with regards to judging others.'

To provide her with even greater quiet, generous supporters built a nice bungalow for her in the palm-tree forest of the monastery garden. However, before long her moods changed. She suffered internal lack and noticed that she could not possibly meditate all day long. At the turn of 1955/56 she wrote, that she had reached the end of her wits. She felt relief when the cars of her donors came up the driveway to the monastery and would bring some diversification. Finally, she became even physically ill.

The abbess, Sister Sudhammā, was also a [school] teacher in Colombo. Sister Vajirā found it non-ascetic when a nun was earning money and wrote a critical memorandum in English with her views about the defects of the nun's life. She sent me the text and requested me to make cyclostyle copies of it so that she could distribute it. When I declined, she turned to Mrs. von der Osten, who made the copies of the text. After the polemic pamphlet had been sent out, Vajirā made herself many enemies. They took offence that the stranger, who was living on the alms food of the country, knew everything better. The nuns, for example, switched off the power supply to her kuti and turned a cold shoulder on her. When

I got to hear about it, I approached Ven. Nyānaponika for help, who made an extra effort and went to her and mediated with a lot of difficulties, so that at least she could remain at Biyagāma, now only tolerated with Buddhist equanimity.

Taking on scholastic work offered itself as a way out of her frustration. Having learned English quickly, she then started with intensive Pali studies and soon started to translate texts and carried on a correspondence about Dhamma topics. On her request, I sent her a typewriter.

She once visited Sister Upalavannā, but the two women from Hamburg did not get along with each other. Dr Petri, still a Catholic at the time, wrote to me in his report about his journey to Ceylon, having expressed his reverence for Ven. Nyānatiloka and Ven. Nyānaponika:

> 'With the German postulant Vajirā I could not escape the impression of a rigid and completely unfeminine ambition... It seems that she envisions the founding of a Buddhist nunnery for Europeans following the example of Nyānatiloka, of which she was to become the first abbess. ... She categorically refused to participate in any communal religious activities—not even making exceptions for the sake of doing others a favour.'

One of the dāyakas of the monastery who also donated for her benefit and whom she respected a lot, was Dr. Ananda Nimalasuriya from Colombo. He owned land east of Galle, at Heenatigala near Talpe, in the dry zone, which offered healthier conditions than the coastal zone near Colombo. He got a nice bungalow, a small hermitage, built there, to which she moved in 1959. Young Sinhalese women venerated her very much there, and one lived temporarily with her as a disciple.

In September 1961 I had sent her the first edition of my *Ethik des Buddha*. She replied that especially the description of renunciation was not convincing enough, which was true. She also wrote that she was learning the Dhammapada by heart in Pali and had started with an English translation with the text newly arranged. She also had visited Ven. Nyānaloka on Polgasduwa, and complained about the oppressive climate. Wolfgang Seel had written to her in September 1961 and had criticised her a lot. She did not reply. In any case, correspondence with German Buddhists, I included, faded away in 1961. Only with Mrs. von der Osten she continued corresponding.

Ven. Ñāṇavīra Thera in front of his *kuti* in Bundala. January, 1965.

Around autumn of 1961 the English monk Ven. Ñāṇavīra Thera, who lived 40 km from her in a kuti in the jungle as a hermit, had sent both to me and to her, a text he had written, *A Note on Paṭicca Samuppāda*, wherein he criticized the extension over three-lives interpretation. Vajirā had briefly met him and his friend Ven. Nyānamoli at the Vajirārāma monastery in Colombo in 1955. About that she wrote this to Germany at the time:

> 'I was told that he tried to live in solitude in the mountains, because he is a great friend of meditation; however he had to return because he did not get enough to live on.'[68]

In 1956 Ven. Ñāṇavīra had written an article called 'A Proof of Rebirth'[69] in the *Buddha Jayanthi* magazine, which was published in Colombo to commemorate the 2500th anniversary of Buddhism. Vajirā liked it so much that she translated it into German and sent it to Max Ladner in November 1956.[70] He agreed to publish it in the magazine *Die Einsicht*. However, Ven. Ñānavīra did not agree with the translation and publication which in the end didn't take place.[71]

On 12 November 1961 she thanked Ven. Ñāṇavīra for sending the Note, 'which could have been written for me,' for a letter of 9 November 1961 and notified him that she would like to meet him on Polgasduwa, where he was staying for a few days, to talk about his text. On 18 November 1961 she arranged that her supporters bring her there by car early in the morning. A conversation which lasted for several hours took place on the island. Thereupon an intensive exchange of letters followed. She wrote sixteen more long letters, the last one on 25 January 1962. His letters she burned, for which she apologised: 'That I burnt your letters and notes was the most dangerous act that I ever committed.'

Years later Ven. Ñāṇavīra, who had sent her letters to a friend, wrote about her:

> 'Sister Vajirā is an extremely passionate and self-willed person, with strong emotions, and apparently, something of a visionary ... she alternates between modes-one could almost say attacks-of emotional periods and of admirable clear-headedness ... emotion for her is quite normal, as it is for nearly all women.'

To her last letter, of 25 January 1962, in which she assumed that he controlled the wind-element through breathing exercises, he answered dismissingly on 29 January 1962, saying that the wind-element rather controlled him for the last ten years and disturbed his digestion, so that he could not exercise mindful breathing in and out. This letter was left lying in her kuti for years, until it was discovered after his death.

In the meantime the following had happened. On 5 February 1962 Mrs. Salgado had written to Ven. Ñāṇavīra:

> 'I have to tell you something very sad. Sister Vajirā has gone out of her head. Please do not answer any of her letters on the Dhamma. Some girls have stayed with her for the last few days and came and told Mrs. Nimalasuriya that she is very bad.'

Upon his letter of 7.2. Mrs. Salgado wrote on 12 February:

> 'We went on the 6th and brought sister to Colombo. She ran away in the night from Mrs. Nimalasuriya's house and was walking along the streets, several followed her and with great difficulty

put her into a car. Dr. Nimalasuriya, Dr. Shelton Fernando and their wives along with me forced her into a car and took her to Sulamin Hospital at 2 a.m. … Now she is much better after the treatment; there also, twice she has jumped through the window and roamed about, but the nurse and attendants managed to bring her back. Now Sister Vajirā says that she wants to get into a saree and at times says that she wants to go back to Germany. We are now wondering what to do with her. By this same post I am writing to Rev. Nyānaponika also.'

On 24 February the Sinhalese Siridhamma wrote to Ven. Ñāṇavīra, that they had sent rs. 200-300 worth of clothes for Vajirā:

'Although she was speaking of marriage at one stage, prior to her departure, she had said that she would go back to her foster parents and lead a quiet life (single).'

On 26 February Mrs. Salgado wrote to Ven. Ñāṇavīra:

'Just a line to inform you that Sister Vajirā left for home on the 22nd. She had recovered but not perfectly normal. She was well enough to go by herself, without anyone else to look after her. The Embassy made arrangements for her trip … she gave up her nun's life and became a lay woman. She said that she does not want to be a nun again…'

At around the same time, I got three letters from Ceylon: One from Ven. Nyānaponika in Kandy; one from Ven. Nārada in Colombo; and one from the German embassy there. In this way I was informed about the above developments. The embassy wrote that Ms. Wolf had to be repatriated due to her health situation. Her situation had stabilized to relatively normal, but a ship journey could not be taken into consideration, so that I had to transfer the vouched travel costs for the airplane to the attaché at the embassy. They put her on an airplane and telegraphed me the time of arrival at Hamburg-Fuhlsbüttel. On the morning of 24 February 1962 she arrived. I waited for her in the arrival hall and brought her to the car of Paul Debes, who had also brought his daughter Monika along. The four of us drove to Hannover. The drive over the Elbe bridges was full of obstructions because there was work going on everywhere to repair the damage caused by the flood disaster of 17 February. About her inner flood she only spoke hesitatingly. She had fallen in love with Ven. Ñāṇavīra and had had the feeling that he had come through the air (wind-element) to her in her kuti. On Sunday 5 March I went to Hannover where she was staying with Erika von der Osten. There she spoke about some more things, part of them she told me directly; part of them I heard through Mrs. von der Osten.

On 7 April she moved from Hannover to Hamburg-Fuhlsbüttel, where a Buddhist nature path practitioner, Else Münster, was living in a suburban house together with her brother. They provided Hanna with a spacious loft room, where she was taken care of. I visited her several times there. She told me that she dreamt of Ñāṇavīra every night. Because I did not agree with the opinions about the Dhamma which she expressed, I wrote a dismissive letter to her beginning of June. Apparently that caused another crisis. She declared that Ven. Ñāṇavīra had disrobed, was in London already, and would become King of Ceylon and she the Queen. Yes, that he was already waiting for her in her old house at Heimhuderstrasse. Else Münster quickly decided to take a taxi and bring her there. There she changed her ideas.

While I was on holiday in the Tessin in June-July 1962 she wrote to me that had secretly left the Münster family without saying goodbye and had returned with her suitcase to her foster parents who put her up. That was the beginning of a return to normal. With a lot of effort the foster parents managed to convince her to take up her profession again. And thus she started to work for the textile machine factory Artos in Hamburg on 1 September 1962. Her foster mother died around that time.

End of 1963 I met her and we drove to Rohlfshagen because she wanted to visit Debes one more time, before he went off on his journey to meditate in Burma and Ceylon for more than a year. She had gotten addicted to smoking, had become fat and remarked that she regrettably was only a caricature of herself.

Since I did not hear from her for almost two years, I wanted to visit her in 1964 at her foster father's. She was there, as she said later, but did not open the door. On 2 July 1965 I tried to visit again, met the foster father on the stairs and thus got in. She said that everything seemed to her so far away; she did not really recall whether we had addressed each other in an intimate and casual or in a distant and formal way [in German 'du' or 'Sie', 'you' or 'you']. The inner split could only be overcome very slowly; there were hard battles. She did not want to have anything to do with Buddhism, and she had thrown away all the issues of 'Buddhistische Monatsblätter' [periodical of Buddhist Society Hamburg]. She did not want to visit Mrs. von der Osten, and in any case did not want to have anything to do with women. She maintained that she had not received a copy of Ven. Ñāṇavīra's *Notes on Dhamma*[72] which had been published in the meantime, but she still held him in high esteem. She smoked one cigarette after the other. What she would like to do was travelling and going out.

After[73] her foster father had married a 26 year old woman, whom she did not get along with, she moved to a room in Maschen in 1968, closer to the company she worked for. In 1971 she got a little apartment there[74] and in 1978 her company moved to Maschen, too. Her job was the best therapy for her. She had to get focussed, had to get along with her colleagues and was too tired at night to follow fantasies. Every year she went on a four weeks' holiday in Bavaria. Once she even went to England. Until 1966 she only wore sarees. When her boss forbade her this, she sewed long dresses for herself, which resembled the Indian ones. Her sewing machine was the only 'luxury' in her spartanically equipped apartment without television or telephone. She continued shaving her head and wore a wig. She dismissed requests from Buddhists to meet her. Debes visited her in Maschen one more time.

In 24 March 1986 Samanera Bodhesako had written to her from Ceylon to request permission to publish parts of her letters to Ven. Ñāṇavīra in the planned book *Clearing the Path*. She sent me this letter on 8 April and asked me to inform the Samanero of her agreement[75], which I did on 11 April and added that he could cite her as Sister Vajirā. On 20 March 1988 he wrote me that the book was done and sent out. Also that she, too, had received a copy. On 23 June I answered him that I had read the book with great interest and asked him if he had received a confirmation from her. I did not get a reply to this letter, which also contained some questions and corrections. He had died suddenly in Nepal on 19 August 1988.

On 31 March 1984 Hanna lost her employment at the company for which she had been working for 22 years, because they were reducing personnel. As a compensation she got 32.000 DM. She had never had that much money at one time. She gave in to the temptation to drown the shock of being pensioned in alcohol. Then, however, her Buddhist insight did appeal again: should she wait until her money was used up and she would be forced to stop drinking by external causes? For the time being she reduced it.[76] She radically stopped smoking in 1988.

On 14 February 1989 I went to Maschen and visited Hanna. Most important in the two and a half hours of conversation was her statement that she was still a Buddhist. She had not been in Hamburg since 1978, not even for the burial of her foster father who died in 1982, and who supported her financially until his end.

On the evening of 7 December 1991, she had breathing difficulties, opened the windows of her apartment a bit and sat down at her desk. There her heart failed and she was in another world. That's how she was found two days later. She was buried in nearby Hittfeld.

Revised translation of: Hellmuth Hecker, *Lebensbilder deutscher Buddhisten, Ein bio-bibliographisches Handbuch, Band II: Die Nachfolger*, Konstanz, 1997, chapter 119, p. 374-386. Translation from the German: Ven. Mettiko.

APPENDIX

# A NOTE ON PHASSA[77]

*Ven. Ñāṇavīra Thera*

*Phassa*, 'contact', is defined (*Saḷāyatana Saṃy.* iv,10 (S.iv,67-9)) as the coming together of the eye, forms, and eye-consciousness (and so with the ear and the rest). But it is probably wrong to suppose that we must therefore understand the word *phassa*, primarily at least, as *contact between these three things*.[a] So long as there is *avijjā*, all things (*dhammā*) are fundamentally as described in the earlier part of the *Mūlapariyāyasutta* (*Majjhima* i,1 (M.i,1)); that is to say, they are inherently *in subjection*, they are *appropriated*, they are *mine* (See ANICCA, MAMA, & *NP* (f)). This is the foundation of the notion that *I am* and that *things are in contact with me*. This contact between me and things is *phassa*. The *diṭṭhisampanna* sees the deception, but the *puthujjana* accepts it at its face value and elaborates it into a relationship between *himself* and the *world* (*attā ca loko ca*—which relationship is then capable of further elaboration into a variety of views (*Majjhima* xi,2 (M.ii,233))).[b] But though the *diṭṭhisampanna*

---

**a.** This interpretation of *phassa* is not invited by the *Mahānidānasuttanta* (*Dīgha* ii,2 (D.ii,62)[78]), where *nāmarūpapaccayā phasso* is discussed without reference to *saḷāyatana*, and in terms of *adhivacanasamphassa* and *paṭighasamphassa*. These terms are more easily comprehensible when *phassa* is understood as 'contact between subject and object'. (It is an elementary mistake to equate *paṭighasamphassa* ('resistance-contact') with five-base-contact (*cakkhusamphassa* &c.) and *adhivacanasamphassa* ('designation-contact') with mind-contact (*manosamphassa*). *Adhivacana* and *paṭigha* correspond to *nāma* and *rūpa* respectively, and it is clear from *Majjhima* iii,8 (M.i,190-1)[79] that both *nāma and rūpa* are conditions for each of the six kinds of contact. See NĀMA.)

**b.** The *puthujjana* takes for granted that 'I am' is the fundamental fact, and supposes that 'things are mine (*or* concern me) *because* I am'. The *diṭṭhisampanna* sees that this is the wrong way round. He sees that there is the conceit (concept) '(I) am' *because* 'things are mine'. With perception of impermanence, the inherent appropriation subsides; 'things are mine' gives place to just 'things are' (which things are still *significant*—they point to or indicate other things—, but no longer point to a 'subject'); and 'I am' vanishes. With the coming to an end of the *arahat*'s life there is the ending of 'things are'. While the *arahat* still lives, then, there continue is not deceived, yet until he becomes *arahat* the aroma of subjectivity (*asmī ti*, '(I) am') hangs about all his experience. All normal experience is dual (*dvayaṃ*—see NĀMA, final paragraph): there are present (i) one's conscious six-based body (*saviññāṇaka saḷāyatanika kāya*), and (ii) other phenomena (namely, whatever is *not* one's body); and reflexion will show that, though both are objective in the experience, the aroma of subjectivity that attaches to the experience will naturally tend to be attributed to the body.[a] In this way, *phassa* comes to be seen as contact between the conscious eye and forms—but mark that this is *because* contact is *primarily* between subject and object, and not between eye, forms, and eye-consciousness. This approach makes it possible to see in what sense, with the entire cessation of all illusion of 'I' and 'mine', there is *phassanirodha* in the *arahat* (where, though there are still, so long as he continues to live, both the conscious body and the other phenomena, there is no longer any appropriation). But when (as commonly) *phassa* is interpreted as 'contact between sense-organ and sense-object, resulting

---

to be 'objects' in the sense of 'things'; but if 'objects' are understood as necessarily correlative to a 'subject', then 'things' can no longer be called 'objects'. See ATTĀ. Similarly with the 'world' as the correlative of 'self': so long as the *arahat* lives, there is still an organized perspective of significant things; but they are no longer significant 'to him', nor do they 'signify him'. See Preface (f).

**a.** If experience were confined to the use of a single eye, the eye and forms would not be distinguishable, they would not appear as separate things; there would be just the experience describable in terms of *pañc'upādānakkhandhā*. But normal experience is always multiple, and other faculties (touch and so on) are engaged at the same time, and the eye and forms as separate things are manifest to them (in the duality of experience already referred to). The original experience is thus found to be a *relationship*: but the fleshly eye is observed (by the other faculties, notably touch, and by the eyes themselves seeing their own reflexion) to be invariable (it is always 'here', *idha*), whereas forms are observed to be variable (they are plural and 'yonder', *huraṃ*). Visual experience, however, also is variable, and its entire content is thus naturally attributed to forms and none of it to the eye. In visual experience, then, *forms are seen, the eye is unseen*, yet (as our other faculties or a looking-glass informs us) *there is the eye*. Also in visual experience, *but in quite a different way* (indicated earlier), *objects are seen, the subject is unseen* (explicitly, at least; otherwise it (or he) would be an object), yet *there is the subject* ('*I am*'). On account of their structural similarity these two independent patterns appear one superimposed on the other; and when there is failure to distinguish between these patterns, *the subject comes to be identified with the eye* (and *mutatis mutandis* for the other *āyatanāni*). See VIÑÑĀṆA for an account of how, in a similar way, consciousness comes to be superimposed on the eye (and the six-based body generally).

in consciousness'—and its translation as '(sense-)impression' implies this interpretation—then we are at once cut off from all possibility of understanding *phassanirodha* in the *arahat*;[a] for the question whether or not the eye is the subject is not even raised—we are concerned only with the eye as a sense-organ, and it is a sense-organ in *puthujjana* and *arahat* alike. Understanding of *phassa* now consists in accounting for consciousness starting from physiological (or neurological) descriptions of the sense-organs and their functioning. Consciousness, however, is not physiologically observable, and the entire project rests upon unjustifiable assumptions from the start.[b] This epistemological interpretation of *phassa*

---

a. *Phusanti phassā upadhiṃ paṭicca*
*Nirūpadhiṃ kena phuseyyuṃ phassā.*[80] *Udāna* ii,4 (Ud.12)
It must, of course, be remembered that *phassanirodha* in the *arahat* does not mean that experience as such (*pañcakkhandhā*) is at an end. But, also, there is no experience without *phassa*. In other words, to the extent that we can still speak of an eye, of forms, and of eye-consciousness (seeing)—e.g. *Saṃvijjati kho āvuso Bhagavato cakkhu, passati Bhagavā cakkhunā rūpaṃ, chandarāgo Bhagavato n'atthi, suvimuttacitto Bhagavā*[81] (*Saḷāyatana Saṃy.* xviii,5 (S.iv,164))—to that extent we can still speak of *phassa*. But it must no longer be regarded as contact with *me* (or with *him*, or with *somebody*). There is, and there is not, contact in the case of the *arahat*, just as there is, and there is not, consciousness. See CETANĀ (f).

b. The reader may note that the word 'sensation' is claimed by physiology: a sensation is what is carried by, or travels over, the nervous system. One respectable authority speaks 'in physiological terms alone' of 'the classical pathways by which sensation reaches the thalamus and finally the cerebral cortex'. Presumably, therefore, a sensation is an electro-chemical impulse in a nerve. But the word properly belongs to psychology: Sensation, according to the *Pocket Oxford Dictionary*, is 'Consciousness of perceiving or seeming to perceive some state or affection of one's body or its parts or senses or of one's mind or its emotions'. What, then, is sensation—is it nervous impulse? or is it consciousness? Or is it not, rather, a convenient verbal device for persuading ourselves that consciousness *is* nervous impulse, and therefore physiologically observable? 'Consciousness' affirms our authority 'is the sum of the activities of the whole nervous system', and this appears to be the current official doctrine.

The notion of *sensation*, however, as we see from the dictionary's definition, is an abomination from the start—how can one 'perceive the state of one's senses' when it is precisely *by means* of one's senses that one perceives? (See MANO.) Another individual's perception (with *his* eye) of the state of my eye may well have, in certain respects, a one-one correspondence with my perception (with *my* eye) of, say, a tree (or, for that matter, a ghost, or, since the eye as visual organ extends into the brain, a migraine); but it is mere lazy thinking to presume from this that when I perceive a tree I am *really* perceiving the state of my eye—and misconceives the Dhamma as a kind of natural-science-cum-psychology that provides an *explanation* of things in terms of cause-and-effect.

---

then, to account for my sensation, *inferring* the existence of a tree in a supposed 'external' world beyond my experience. The reader is referred to Sartre's excellent discussion of this equivocal concept (*op. cit.*, pp. 372-8), of which we can give here only the peroration. *'La sensation, notion hybride entre le subjectif et l'objectif, conçue à partir de l'objet, et appliquée ensuite au sujet, existence bâtarde dont on ne saurait dire si elle est de fait ou de droit, la sensation est une pure rêverie de psychologue, il faut la rejeter délibérément de toute théorie sérieuse sur les rapports de la conscience et du monde.'* ('Sensation, hybrid notion between the subjective and the objective, conceived starting from the object, and then applied to the subject, bastard entity of which one cannot say whether it is *de facto* or *de jure*,—sensation is a pure psychologist's day-dream: it must be deliberately rejected from every serious theory on the relations of consciousness [which, for Sartre, is subjectivity] and the world.') Descartes, it seems, with his 'representative ideas', is the modern philosopher primarily responsible for the present tangle—see Heidegger, *op. cit.*, p. 200 *et seq.* (Heidegger quotes Kant as saying that it is 'a scandal of philosophy and of human reason in general' that there is still no cogent proof for the 'being-there of things outside us' that will do away with all scepticism. Then he remarks 'The "scandal of philosophy" is not that this proof is yet to be given, but that *such proofs are expected and attempted again and again*'.) Removal of the pseudo-problem of the 'external' world removes materialism, but does not remove matter (for which see NĀMA & RŪPA).

# EDITORIAL NOTES

1. **'Sketch for a Proof of Rebirth'**: This 15.000-word essay was reprinted several times in abridged form. The typescript found among the author's papers contains a number of pencilled comments indicating later disagreement with his earlier views. See *StP*.

2. **Note on Paṭicca Samuppāda and Paramatha Sacca**: both published in *NoD*, Path Press Publications, 2009, p. 25-33.

3. **rough draft**: See L. 149/159.

4. **essay**: See *NoD*, A NOTE ON PAṬICCASAMUPĀDA, p. 1-23

5. **Jīvaka Sutta:** Ven. Ñāṇavīra's letter to Mrs. Perera of 26 October 1961 includes. '... the Sutta in question is the Jīvaka Sutta (of the Majjhima, M.55/i,369). This Sutta does not prohibit people from eating meat, but says that *bhikkhus* may not eat meat that they have seen, heard, or suspected as having been killed on their account.' (*CtP*, 2010, L.6)

6. **a note on *sūkara-maddava***: See note 46 of *Last Days of the Buddha* (Wheel 67-69, second edition 1974): '*sūkara-maddava*: a controversial term which has therefore been left untranslated. *Sūkara* = pig; *maddava* = soft, tender, delicate. Hence two alternative renderings of the compound are possible: (1) the tender parts *of* a pig or boar; (2) what is enjoyed *by* pigs and boars. In the latter meaning, the term has been thought to refer to a mushroom or truffle, or a yam or tuber. K.E. Neumann, in the preface to his German translation of the Majjhima Nikāya, quotes from an Indian compendium of medicinal plants, the *Rājanigaṇṭu*, several plants beginning with *sūkara*: *sūkarakaṇḍa*, *sūkariṭṭas* ('desired by pigs'), etc.
The commentary to our text gives three alternative explanations:

(1) the flesh from a single first-born (wild) pig, neither too young nor too old, which had come to hand naturally (*pavattamaṃsa*), i.e., without intentional killing; (2) a preparation of soft boiled rice cooked with the five cow-products; (3) a kind of alchemistic elixir (*rasāyanavidhi*).—Dhammapāla, in his commentary to Udāna VIII, 5, gives, in addition to explanation (1)-(3): "young bamboo shoots trampled by pigs" (*sūkarehi maddita-vaṃsa-kaḷīro*).'
*Sūkara-maddava* is with Franke (*Dīghanikāya*, 1913, p. 222 sq.) to be interpreted as 'soft (tender) boar's flesh'. So also Oldenberg (*Reden des Buddha*, 1922, p. 109) & Fleet (J.R.A.S. 1906, p. 656 & p. 881). Scarcely with Rhys Davids (*Dialogues of the Buddha*, II, p. 137, with note) as 'quantity of truffles', D. ii,127; Ud. 81 sq.; Miln. 175.

7. ***Muhuttam...***:
Even though, for a brief moment,
an intelligent one attends on a wise person,
he quickly perceives dhamma,
as the tongue, the flavor of the dish.
Dhp. 65 (translation by John Ross Carter and Mahinda Palihawadana, Oxford University Press, 1987, p. 151)

8. ***parato...***: 'Another's utterance and proper attention. These, monks, are the two conditions for the arising of right view' (Aṅguttara II, xi, 9).

9. **ripeness is all**: See Shakespeare, *King Lear*.

10. ***upāsikā***: See the P.S. to L. 100/107, p. 91.

11. ***paṭiccasamuppāda***: See *NoD*, NOTE ON PAṬICCASAMUPPĀDA, p. 1-23.

12. ***Evam eva kho...***: 'Just so, Māgandiya, if I were to set you forth the Teaching, "This is that good health, this is that extinction," you might know good health, you might see extinction; with the arising of the eye, that in the five holding aggregates which is desire-&-lust would be eliminated for you; moreover it would occur to you, "For

a long time, indeed, have I been cheated and deceived and defrauded by this mind (or heart—*citta*): I was holding just matter, holding just feeling, holding just perception, holding just determinations, holding just consciousness."' See *NoD*, PARAMATTHA SACCA §4.

13. *yo pañcas'...*: 'in the five holding aggregates which is desire-&-lust, that therein is holding.' See *NoD*, PARAMATTHA SACCA §3.

14. *yam kiñci...*: 'Whatever has the nature of arising, all that has the nature of ceasing.'

15. *sati vā...*: 'Or, if there is a remainder, non-returning'.

16. **Itivuttaka 44/38**: Bhikkhus, there are these two Nibbāna-elements. What are the two? The Nibbāna-element with residue left and the Nibbāna-element with no residue left. What, bhikkhus, is the Nibbāna-element with residue left? Here a bhikkhu is an arahant, one whose taints are destroyed, the holy life fulfilled, who has done what had to be done, laid down the burden, attained the goal, destroyed the fetters of being and is completely released through final knowledge. However, his five sense qualities remain unimpaired, by which he still experiences what is agreeable and disagreeable and feels pleasure and pain. It is the extinction of attachment [greed], hate and delusion in him that is called Nibbāna-element with residue left.
Now what, bhikkhus, is the Nibbāna-element with no residue left? Here a bhikkhu is an arahant [...] completely released through final knowledge. For him, here in this very life, all that is experienced, not being delighted in, will be extinguished. That, bhikkhus, is called the Nibbāna-element with no residue left.
(Translation from John D. Ireland, *The Itivuttaka, The Buddha's Sayings*, BPS, 1991.)

17. *catunnam...*: 'and matter held (i.e. taken up by craving) from the four great entities.' See *NoD*, Additional Texts 78.

18. *taṇhupādiṇṇa...*: 'the body, taken up by craving'.

19. **undated**: But apparently in response to a letter dated 20 November 1961.

20. See Ven. Ñāṇavīra Thera's letter of 21 November 1961 [L. 146/156].

21. ***sammādiṭṭhi...***: 'Right view that is noble, taintless, beyond the world, a factor of the path.' Mahācattārīsaka Sutta—M.117/iii,72.

22. ***Tathāgato...***: 'Tahthāgata enters Parinibbāna the extinction-element without residue.' Mahāparinibbāna Sutta—D.16/ii,108-9.

23. ***saññā-vedayita-nirodha***: 'cessation of perception and feeling'.

24. ***Dukkha-nirodha-gāmini Paṭipadā***: 'Leading to the cessation of suffering.'

25. ***parāmaṭṭha***: 'misapprehended (i.e. *sīla* of which more is expected than it is capable of providing, as, e.g. go-*sīla*, or *sīla* in a *puthujjana* who has no *sammādiṭṭhi*)' (Bhikkhu Ñāṇamoli, *A Pali-English Glossary of Buddhist Technical Terms*, BPS, 1994).

26. ***sammādiṭṭhi pubbaṅgama***: 'Right view comes first.'

27. **Okkantika Saṃy.**: See note 31.

28. **Kisāgotamī Theri**: Thīg. 10.1 (143).

29. ***Anaññāte aññatamānī***: 'One who prides himself in having perfect knowledge, not in reference to the unknown'. Dutiyasammattaniyāma Sutta—A.V.ii.152/iii,174.

30. ***ubhato-bhāga-vimutta***: 'liberated in both ways'.

31. ***Magga-Phala***: Ven. Ñāṇavīra's view on *magga-* and *phala-*attainments can be found in CITTA, *NoD*, p. 45-46: "Connected with this doctrine is the erroneous notion of *anuloma-gotrabhu-magga-phala*, supposed to be the successive moments in the attainment of *sotāpatti*. It is sometimes thought that the word *akālika* as applied to

the Dhamma means that attainment of *magga* is followed 'without interval of time' by attainment of *phala*; but this is quite mistaken. *Akālika dhamma* has an entirely different meaning (for which see PAṬICCASAMUPPĀDA). Then, in the *Okkantika Saṃyutta* (S.iii, 225) it is stated only that the *dhammānusārī* and the *saddhānusārī* (who have reached the *magga* leading to *sotāpatti*) are bound to attain *sotāpattiphala* before their death; and other Suttas—e.g. *Majjhima* vii,5&10 (M.i,439&479)—show clearly that one is *dhammānusārī* or *saddhānusārī* for more than 'one moment'. For *gotrabhu* see *Majjhima* xiv,12 (M.iii,256), where it says that he may be *dussīla pāpadhamma*. In Sutta usage it probably means no more than 'a member of the *bhikkhusaṅgha*'.

32. ***Evam etaṃ...***: 'In this way the wise see action as it really is, seeing dependent arising, understanding result of action.' Suttanipāta 653. See also KAMMA in *NoD*, p. 43.

33. ***idameva...***: 'Only this is true, other things are false'.

34. ***catunnaṃ...***: 'Matter held (i.e. taken up by craving) from the four great entities.' Sabbāsava Sutta—M.9/i,9.

35. ***chandajāto...***:
'One in whom a wish for the Undefined is born,
Who would be clear in mind,
Whose heart is not bound in sensual pleasures,
Is called 'one whose stream is upward bound.'
Dhp. 218 (translation by John Ross Carter and Mahinda Palihawadana, Oxford University Press, 1987, p. 267.)

36. ***Nava anupubba-nirodhā***: 'Nine successive cessations.' See Saṅgīti Sutta—D.33/iii,266.

37. Presumably paragraph II of this letter, the existing portion of which was copied from the back of the last page of Sister Vajirā's letter. The remainder of the letter is lost.
'The last sentence of para II' seems to refer to the second paragraph of L. 149/159 (which predates Sister Vajirā's request by about ten

days) and which itself seems to refer to PHASSA [d] (See the Appendix). It will be noticed that most of the draft reproduced here is, in the event, an early version of the third paragraph of ATTĀ. In fact, a considerable part of the *SN* in *NoD* seems to be material reworked from those letters to Sister Vajirā which 'perished in the great flames'.

38. **passage**: See the Appendix.

39. Remainder of this letter is missing.

40. *Note on Phassa*: See the Appendix.

41. ***yaṃ kiñci...***: 'Whatever is felt counts as unpleasure (suffering).' Nidāna/Abhisamaya Saṃy. iv,2.

42. ***paṭiccasamuppādadasā kammavipākakovidā***: See note 32.

43. ***Anuvicca...***:
'Knowing diversification of name-and-matter
the root of disease, internal and external,
one, freed from fetters, the root of all disease,
is rightly called "one who knows well".'

44. ***Na saññasaññī...***:
'Neither perceiving perception, nor not-perceiving perception,
neither without perception, nor with perception of what is gone.
For one who has attained to such a state matter ceases,
for the calculation of diversification has its origin in perception.'

45. ***Mūlaṃ...***:
'Being a wise man, he would stop
the whole root of calculation of diversification: '(I) am'.
Whatever internal cravings there are
he, always mindful, would train himself for dispelling them.'

46. ***khīṇāsavā...***: 'one whose cankers are destroyed, knower of the Uncreated, victor, detached from the world, one who has done, one

who has put down his burden, without any clinging, completely calmed, one who wears his last body, free from passions, unshakable.'

47. **Kevaddha Sutta**: In this Sutta the Buddha tells the story of the bhikkhu who wanted to know 'Where do the four great elements finally cease.' With meditation he went into heavens, but none there could tell him, not even the Mahā Brahmā, who referred him back to the Buddha for an answer.

48. ***Yaṃ kiñci...***: 'Any kind of form: past, future, present; internal or external; gross or subtle; inferior or superior, far or in the presence, [he sees] all form thus: "This is mine, this am I, this is my self."' (The passage not found in the Pali Suttas.)

49. ***avijjāgato...***: 'If, bhikkhus, this individual, who is involved in ignorance (nescience), is determining a meritorious determination, [consciousness has arrived at merit; if he is determining a demeritorious determination, consciousness has arrived at demerit]; if he determining an imperturbable determination, consciousness has arrived imperturbable.' Nidāna Saṃy., Parivīmaṃsana Sutta—S.xii.51/ii,82.

50. ***paññāya vā adhimuccati***: 'He is inclined to wisdom.' Āneñjasappāya Sutta—M.106/ii,262.

51. ***Idh'ānanda...***: 'Here, Ānanda, a bhikkhu is practising thus: 'If it were not, it would not be mine; [it will not be and it will not be mine. What exists, what has come to be, that I am abandoning.' Thus he obtains equanimity. He delights in that equanimity, welcomes it, and remains holding to it. As he does so,] his consciousness dependent on it and holds to it. As he does so, his consciousness becomes dependent on it and holds to it. A bhikkhu, Ānanda, who is effected by holding does not attain extinction.
But, venerable sir, when that bhikkhu holds, what does he hold to?
To the base of neither-perception-nor-non-perception, Ānanda.
[...] Here, Ānanda, a noble disciple considers thus: 'Sensual pleasures here and now [and sensual pleasures in lives to come, sensual

perceptions here and now and sensual perceptions in lives to come, material forms here and now and material forms in lives to come, perceptions of forms here and now and perceptions of forms in lives to come, perceptions of the imperturbable, perceptions of the base of nothingness,] and perceptions of the base of neither-perception-nor-non-perception—this is personality as far as personality extends, this is the Deathless, namely, the liberation of the mind through not holding.' Āneñjasappāya Sutta—M.106/ii,264-5 (translation from Bhikkhu Ñāṇamoli, Bhikkhu Bodhi, *The Middle Length Discourses of the Buddha*, Wisdom Publications, 1995, p. 872)

52. *Etaṃ mama...*: 'This is mine, this am I, this is my self.' Alagaddūpama Sutta—M.22/i,135.

53. **S. iv,384**: 'since here and now the Tathāgata actually and in truth is not to be found.' See PARAMATTHA SACCA §4 [a].

54. **Thīg. 106**: 'The five aggregates, being completely known, stand with the root cut off.'

55. *anejo...*: 'A mindful bhikkhu may wonder about unshaken, without holding on.' Sn. 751.

56. **Sīvaka Sutta**: The draft did not include a translation of this Sutta, which is provided here by the editors.

57. *Tassa me...* : It is likely that the letter sent to Sister Vajirā contained a more extensive extract from this discourse, wherein Ven. Udāyi tells the Buddha that his strong reverence for the Buddha has done much for him. 'The Auspicious One taught Dhamma to me: "This is matter, this is the arising of matter, this is the ceasing of matter...".' Ven. Udāyi relates how he then went into solitude and, reflecting on the fluctuations and vicissitudes of the five aggregates, he came to realize as it really is suffering, suffering's arising, suffering's ceasing, and the path leading to the ceasing of suffering. 'Then, lord, I fully understood Dhamma and attained the Path.' Having become *sotāpanna*, Ven. Udāyi then understood the way which would lead him to extinction.

58. *sabbe sattā...*: It seems that the passage is combined from two places in *Sangīti Sutta*: *sabbe sattā saṅkhāra-ṭṭhitikā*: 'all beings are dependent by determinations' (D.iii,211); and *cha sañcetanā-kāyā*: 'six groups of intention' (D.iii,244).

59. *anulomikāya khantiyā samannāgato*: 'endowed with acquiescence in conformity'. See *NoD*, SAKKĀYA (b), pp. 84-5: 'such an individual is not at contrary view to the Teaching, but does not actually see it for himself'. It seems that Ven. Ñāṇavīra still doubted of Sister Vajirā's attainments.

60. **individual**: Paul Debes.

61. *anatimānī*: non-arogance. Sister Vajirā may have had in mind the first verse of the well-known Mettā Sutta (Discourse on Friendliness), Sn. 143: 'One skilled as to the goal, having entered upon the way of peace, should do this: he should be capable, straight, upright, of good speech, gentle, non-arrogant.'

62. **these**: or 'there'; illegible in MS.

63. *Sammattaniyāmaṃ okkanti*: 'entry into surety of correctness'. See A. VI,86/iii,435 & 449.

64. **Sunakkhatta Sutta**: M.105. The Buddha's Teaching on the problem of an individual's overestimations of his practice.

65. *Yo...*: 'He who sees dependent arising sees the Teaching. He who sees the Teaching sees me.' The first sentence is ascribed to the Buddha by the Ven. Sāriputta at M.28/i,190-191. The second sentence is spoken by the Buddha at Khandha Saṃy.—S.xxii.87/iii,120.)

66. This letter, not included in the first edition of *CtP* (Path Press, 1987), was found around 1989 by a nun living in the south of Sri Lanka. Apparently, this letter, the existence of which was not previously known, had remained in Vajirā's kuti for some 27 years untouched—except by insects and mold—until she found it.

67. Hellmuth Hecker (1923) lives in Hamburg. He is a leading German writer on buddhism and translator from the Pali Canon. His books include a German translation of the Saṃyutta Nikāya (parts 4 and 5), a two-volume chronicle on buddhism in Germany, and a biography of Ven. Nyanatiloka Mahathera, the first German buddhist monk.

68. Ven. Ñāṇavīra in 1954 and 1955 moved from the Island Hermitage to various places, trying to find a remote section of Ceylon in order to practice. He was living on mountains and in caves and still probably came back to the Island Hermitage from time to time (See *StP*).

69. The article appears also in forthcoming *StP*.

70. On 17 November 1956 Sister Vajirā wrote to Max Ladner:

Lieber Herr Ladner,
Ich sende Ihnen hier eine Uebersetzung des Artikels 'The Proof of Rebirth', der kuerzlich in der hiesigen Zeitschrift 'Buddha Jayanti' erschien und mir wegen der ausgezeichneten Behandlung dieses allgemein interessanten Themas in die Augen fiel. Ich wuerde mich freuen, wenn Sie ihn in der 'Einsicht' veroeffentlichen koennten, weil ich glaube, dass er vielen Lesern viel sagen wurde.
Ich habe natuerlich die Erlaubnis des Autors, indirekt durch Nyaponika, Thero, und des Verlages eingeholt. N., Thero, teilte mir mit, dass er Ihnen ein Exemplar der Zeitschrift zugesendt hatte. Der Titel, wie er in meine Uebersetzung gegeben ist, ist der vom Autor eigentlich beabsichtigte. Ich habe die vielen Klammern durch Worte ersetzt, weil ich sie irritierend finde. Das einleitende Zitat habe ich im Moment nicht in der Uebersetzung hier und moechte es nicht selbst uebersetzen, vielleicht fuegen Sie es in der Uebersetzung des Mahatheras (ich glaube, im 'Wort des Buddha' zu finden) ein.
Sollten Sie kein Interesse haben, den Aufsatz zu veroeffentlichen, dann senden Sie ihn bitte Herr. Dr. Hecker. Was ist aus meinem damaligen Aufsatz ueber 'Die vier Arten der Unterweisung' geworden? Ich hoerte vor einiger Zeit, dass sie ihn veroeffentlichen wollten, was mir sehr freuen wuerde. Er ist ein bisschen lang, nicht wahr?

Gruessen Sie alle buddhistische Freunde herzlich von mir.
Mettā cittena
Vajirā[a]

71. On 14 December 1956 Sister Vajirā wrote to Max Ladner:

Lieber Herr Ladner,
Besten Dank fuer Ihre freundlichen Zeile und Einlage. Ich bin einigermassen erstaunt ueber die Entwicklung dieser Angelegenheit. Jedenfalls ist dies eine sehr seltsame Reaktionsweise des englischen Bhikkhus auf meinen anerkennenden Brief hin. Er muss gedacht haben, ich haette alles, was in den Klammern zum Ausdruck kommt, ausgelassen, waerend ich nur die Klammern selbst ausgelassen hatte. Ich kennen ihn gar nicht persoenlich, ausser, dass ich ihn ein paarmal im Vajirārāma in Colombo gesehen habe, und er hat mir auf meinen Brief nicht geantwortet. Rein nach dem Essay hatte ich schon das Empfinden, dass er pedantisch sei, was sich also als richtig erweist.
Na ja, die ist eine gute Lektion fuer mich. Man soll sich eben nicht mit der Welt einlassen, nicht einmal bis zu diesem Grade. –

---

**a.** Dear Mr. Ladner,
Herewith I send you a translation of the article 'The Proof of Rebirth' which was recently published in the local periodical 'Buddha Jayanti' and that caught my attention because of the excellent treatment of this subject of general interest. I would be glad if you could publish it in 'Der Einsicht' because I believe it has great value to most of the readers.

Of course I received permission of the author, indirectly through Nyanaponika, Thero, and the publisher. N., Thero told me he send you a copy of the issue. The title, as it appears in my translation, is what the author wanted it to be. I have replaced the many brackets with words, because I found them irritating. At the moment I don't have a translation of the preliminary quotation, and I didn't want to translate it myself; you might be able to add it in the translation of the Mahathera (I believe you can find it in his 'Wort des Buddha').

If you have no interest in publishing the essay, than please send it to Mr. Dr. Hecker. What has become of my earlier essay about 'The Four Ways of Teaching'? Some time ago I heard that you wanted to publish it, what would make me very happy. It's a bit long, isn't it?
Greetings to all buddhist friends.
Mettā cittena
Vajirā

Die Sympathie und das Verstaendnis, die Sie fuer meine Absicht aufbringen, sind dankenswert. Es ist jedoch sehr schade, dass sie das Essay nicht drucken wollen, weil Sie ueber den Wert dessen anderer Meinung sind. Es liegt mir fern, mich in ein Wortgefecht einzulassen, obgleich ich Ihre Gruende gegen den Aufsatz nicht stichhaltig finde, der Bhikkhu wird wohl selbst der best Verfechter seiner Ideen sein, es hat den Anschein, dass wir auf diesem Gebiet schwerlich zu einer Uebereinstimmung kommen koennen.
Fuer mich ist dieser Artikel das, was er zu sein beabsichtigt, ein sehr subtiler aber schlagender Beweis, was ich selbst frueher fuer unmoeglich hielt. Alles andere, was ich bisher zu diesem Thema – was mich, nebenbei gesagt, gar nicht interessiert, weil es mir selbstverstandlich ist – gelesen habe, ist wirklich blosses Gerede, aber dies nicht. –
Was ich immer, auch bei Paul Debes, bei dem Herausgeber einer Zeitschrift vermisse, ist Toleranz. Es muessen doch nicht nur die Meinungen des Editors zur Sprache kommen, sondern, da wir ja alle so sehr unterschiedlich sind, sollte so eine Zeitschrift viele Moeglichkeiten bieten, das wuerde ihr nur zum Vorteil gereichen. Sicher, ein verantwortungsbewusster Regulator muss da sein, und dies beides mag zuweilen schwer zu vereinbaren sein. Ich denke z.B., dass dieser Aufsatz niemals zur Konfusion beitragen kann, waehrend viele Artikel der 'Einsicht' dies tun.
Was meinen Aufsatz betrifft, so wuesste ich nicht, was man da kuerzen koennte, weshalb mir eine Kuerzung auch nicht lieb waere. Koennen Sie ihn nicht vielleicht in vier Teilen erscheinen lassen? Das haette natuerlich auch viele Nachteile. Am Besten waere er als Sonderdruck, da es sich hierbei um die Behandlung eines bestimmten Lehrkomplexes handelt. Sonst lassen sie ihn nur ganz beiseite, und senden Sie ihn bitte an Dr. Hecker.
Mit den besten Wuenschen fuer Ihr Wohlergehen,
Mettā cittena
Vajirā[a]

---

**a.** Dear Mr. Ladner,
Thank you very much for your kind lines and attachment. I'm a little bit surprised with how this case develops. Anyhow, this is a very strange way of reacting of the English bhikkhu to my recognizing letter. He must have thought that I

72. It is a first edition (1963). Ven. Ñāṇavīra later updated and extented the book.

73. Dr. Helmuth Hecker had not seen her for 22 years, from 1965 until 1987. The following information he got from a Elisabeth Körtke who also got information from others who knew Hanna. That part of Hanna's life is quite unknown since, as Elisabeth recall, 'she never told something' and 'she was absolutely single person and had no friends.' Elisabeth remembers: 'She went very slowly, she laughed often and the other peoples didn't understand the reason why. The first time, when she worked as a technician designer, she was very clever. Slow, but clever... She was never on time.' Also apparently she never visited theatres or concert halls. 'My personal feeling is

---

deleted everything what was expressed between brackets, while I only deleted the brackets themselves. I don't know him personally, except that I have seen him a few times at the Vajirārāma in Colombo, and he didn't answer my letter. Already the essay gave me the impression he is rather pedantic, what seems to be true. I consider it a good lesson for me. One shouldn't interfere with the world, not even so much as this. –

The sympathy and understanding you have for my work is praiseworthy. But it is very sad that you are not willing to publish the essay, because you think differently about its value. I have no interest at all in fighting with words, but while I find the reasons you have against the essay not valid, the Bhikkhu is himself the best defender of his ideas, it seems we won't be able to find an agreement about this.

For me the article is what it intents to be, a subtle but convincing proof, something I thought to be impossible. Everything else what I have read about it –what doesn't interest me at all, because for me it is evident – is really idle talk; but this isn't.

The one thing a magazine publisher always lacks is tolerance. Not only the opinions of the editors should be expressed, but, because we are all so different, a magazine should offer a wide range of possibilities, what would make it only more attractive. Of course, a responsible regulator is needed, and both aspects might sometimes be difficult to combine. I think that this article never leads to confusion as a lot of other Einsicht-articles do.

Concerning my own essay, I wouldn't know how to shorten it, what I consider most unwanted. Isn't it possible to publish it in several parts? That also has of course different disadvantages. The best solution would be a separate release, because it deals with a single but complex aspect of the Teaching. If not, you can leave it and send it to Dr. Hecker.

With best wishes,
Mettā cittena
Vajirā

that she was a very interesting and exceptional woman, who didn't live in our real world, therefore others couldn't understand her.'

74. Elisabeth describes her place: 'she had her own flat with 2½ rooms, kitchen, bathroom with own furniture. The furniture was very simple: a sofa, where she also slept, 2 cupboards, and an old sewing machine, a writing table and a high fidelity installation. Before that she had only one room. 1975 died my mother and so Hanna got from me some furniture and carpets. TV she refused.'

75. On 8 April 1986 Hanna Wolf wrote to Dr. Hecker:

Maschen, 8th April 1986

My dear Hellmut!
Thank you so much for forwarding the letter from Ceylon. In the same occasion, namely the publication of the book 'Clearing the Path', I would like to ask you friendly, according to the enclosed letter, to communicate there that I am informed about their intentions, and that I do not have any objections towards the publication.
I presume that this will be possible for you. It is a little urgent, too. For a short message in that matter I was grateful.
My especially hearty greetings to Paul Debes, Ingetraut Anderts and family!
Friendly greetings,
your Hanna Wolf

76. This information comes only from Elisabeth Körtke; the editors were unable to get clearer information nor confirmation from others. An example of a *sotāpanna* 'drinking intoxicating drank', see: Sotāpatti Saṃy. LV.24-25/v,375-380. Note that the Sutta is unclear and commentaries have their own interpretation.

77. 'A Note on Phassa' is part of *NoD* (*CtP*, Path Press, 1987, p. 89-92; *NoD*, Path Press Publications, 2009, p. 68-71).

78. ***Dīgha* ii,2:**
*Nāmarūpapaccayā phasso ti iti kho pan'etaṃ vuttaṃ; tad Ānanda iminā p'etaṃ pariyāyena veditabbaṃ yathā nāmarūpapaccayā*

*phasso. Yehi Ānanda ākārehi yehi liṅgehi yehi nimittehi yehi uddesehi nāmakāyassa paññatti hoti, tesu ākāresu tesu liṅgesu tesu nimittesu tesu uddesesu asati, api nu kho rūpakāye adhivacanasamphasso paññāyethā ti.*

*No h'etaṃ bhante.*

*Yehi Ānanda ākārehi yehi liṅgehi yehi nimittehi yehi uddesehi rūpakāyassa paññatti hoti, tesu ākāresu tesu liṅgesu tesu nimittesu tesu uddesesu asati, api nu kho nāmakāye paṭighasamphasso paññāyethā ti.*

*No h'etaṃ bhante.*

*Yehi Ānanda ākārehi yehi liṅgehi yehi nimittehi yehi uddesehi nāmakāyassa ca rūpakāyassa ca paññatti hoti, tesu ākāresu tesu liṅgesu tesu nimittesu tesu uddesesu asati, api nu kho adhivacanasamphasso vā paṭighasamphasso vā paññāyethā ti.*

*No h'etaṃ bhante.*

*Yehi Ānanda ākārehi yehi liṅgehi yehi nimittehi yehi uddesehi nāmarūpassa paññatti hoti, tesu ākāresu tesu liṅgesu tesu nimittesu tesu uddesesu asati, api nu kho phasso paññāyethā ti.*

*No h'etaṃ bhante.*

*Tasmātih'Ānanda es'eva hetu etaṃ nidānaṃ esa samudayo esa paccayo phassassa yadidaṃ nāmarūpaṃ.*

*Viññāṇapaccayā nāmarūpan ti iti kho pan'etaṃ vuttaṃ; tad Ānanda iminā p'etaṃ pariyāyena veditabbaṃ yathā viññāṇapaccayā nāmarūpaṃ. Viññāṇaṃ va hi Ānanda mātu kucchiṃ na okkamissatha, api nu kho nāmarūpaṃ mātu kucchismiṃ samucchissathā ti.*

*No h'etaṃ bhante.*

*Viññāṇaṃ va hi Ānanda mātu kucchiṃ okkamimitvā vokkamissatha, api nu kho nāmarūpaṃ itthattāya abhinibbattissathā ti.*

*No h'etaṃ bhante.*

*Viññāṇaṃ va hi Ānanda daharass'eva sato vocchijjissatha kumārassa vā kumārikāya vā, api nu kho nāmarūpaṃ vuddhiṃ virūlhiṃ vepullaṃ āpajjissathā ti.*

*No h'etaṃ bhante.*

*Tasmātih'Ānanda es'eva hetu etaṃ nidānaṃ esa samudayo esa paccayo nāmarūpassa yadidaṃ viññāṇaṃ.*

*Nāmarūpapaccayā viññāṇan ti iti kho pan'etaṃ vuttaṃ; tad Ānanda iminā p'etaṃ pariyāyena veditabbaṃ yathā nāmarūpapaccayā viññāṇaṃ. Viññāṇaṃ va hi Ānanda nāmarūpa patiṭṭhaṃ nālabhis-*

*satha, api nu kho āyati jātijaramaraṇadukkhasamudayasambhavo paññāyethā ti.*

*No h'etaṃ bhante.*

*Tasmātih'Ānanda es'eva hetu etaṃ nidānaṃ esa samudayo esa paccayo viññāṇassa yadidaṃ nāmarūpaṃ.*

*Ettāvatā kho Ānanda jāyetha vā jīyetha vā mīyetha vā cavetha vā uppajjetha vā, ettāvatā adhivacanapatho, ettāvatā niruttipatho, ettāvatā paññattipatho, ettāvatā paññavacaraṃ, ettāvatā vaṭṭaṃ vaṭṭati itthataṃ paññāpanāya, yadidaṃ nāmarūpaṃ saha viññāṇena.*

—'With name-&-matter as condition, contact', so it was said: how it is, Ānanda, that with name-&-matter as condition there is contact should be seen in this manner. Those tokens, Ānanda, those marks, those signs, those indications by which the name-body is described,—they being absent, would designation-contact be manifest in the matter-body?

—No indeed, lord.

—Those tokens, Ānanda, those marks, those signs, those indications by which the matter-body is described,—they being absent, would resistance-contact be manifest in the name-body?

—No indeed, lord.

—Those tokens, Ānanda, those marks, those signs, those indications by which the name-body and the matter-body are described,—they being absent, would either designation-contact or resistance-contact be manifest?

—No indeed, lord.

—Those tokens, Ānanda, those marks, those signs, those indications by which name-&-matter is described,—they being absent, would contact be manifest?

—No indeed, lord.

—Therefore, Ānanda, just this is the reason, this is the occasion, this is the arising, this is the condition of contact, that is to say name-&-matter.

'With consciousness as condition, name-&-matter', so it was said: how it is, Ānanda, that with consciousness as condition there is name-&-matter should be seen in this manner. If, Ānanda, consciousness were not to descend into the mother's womb, would name-&-matter be consolidated in the mother's womb?

—No indeed, lord.
—If, Ānanda, having desceended into the mother's womb, consciousness were to turn aside, would name-&-matter be delivered into this situation?
—No indeed, lord.
—If, Ānanda, consciousnesss were cut off from one still young, from a boy or a girl, would name-&-matter come to increase, growth, and fullness?
—No indeed, lord.
—Therefore, Ānanda, just this is the reason, this is the occasion, this is the arising, this is the condition of name-&-matter, that is to say consciousness.

'With name-&-matter as condition, consciousness', so it was said: how it is, Ānanda, that with name-&-matter as condition there is consciousness should be seen in this manner. If, Ānanda, consciousness were not to obtain a stay in name-&-matter, would future arising and coming-into-being of birth, ageing, death, and unpleasure (suffering), be manifest?
—No indeed, lord.
—Therefore, Ānanda, just this is the reason, this is the occasion, this is the arising, this is the condition of consciousness, that is to say name-&-matter.

Thus far, Ānanda, may one be born or age or die or fall or arise, thus far is there a way of designation, thus far is there a way of language, thus far is there a way of description, thus far is there a sphere of understanding, thus far the round proceeds as manifestation in a situation,—so far, that is to say, as there is name-&-matter together with consciousness.

79. ***Majjhima* iii,8:**
*Yato ca kho āvuso ajjhattikañ c'eva cakkhuṃ [sotaṃ, ghānaṃ, jivhā, kāyo, mano] aparibhinnaṃ hoti, bāhirā ca rūpā [saddā, gandhā, rasā, phoṭṭhabbā, dhammā] āpāthaṃ āgacchanti, tajjo ca samannāhāro hoti, evaṃ tajjassa viññāṇabhāgassa pātubhāvo hoti. Yaṃ tathābhūtassa rūpaṃ taṃ rūp'upādānakkhandhe saṅgahaṃ gacchati; ...vedanā...; ...saññā...; ...saṅkhārā...; yaṃ tathābhūtassa viññāṇaṃ taṃ viññāṇ'upādānakkhandhe saṅgahaṃ gacchati.*

It is when, friends, the internal eye (ear, nose, tongue, body, mind) is unbroken, and external visible forms (sounds, smells, tastes, touches, images/ideas) come in the way, and there is the appropriate connexion,—it is then that there is the appearance of the appropriate kind of consciousness. Of what thus comes into existence, the matter goes for inclusion in the holding aggregate of matter; ...the feeling...; ...the perception...; ...the determinations...; of what thus comes into existence, the consciousness goes for inclusion in the holding aggregate of consciousness.

80. *Phusanti...*:
Contacts contact dependent on ground—
How should contacts contact a groundless one?

81. *Saṃvijjati...*:
The Auspicious One, friend, possesses an eye; the Auspicious One sees visible forms with the eye; desire-&-lust for the Auspicious One there is not; the Auspicious One is wholly freed in heart (*citta*).

# GLOSSARY

ALPHABETICAL ORDER IN PALI:
a, ā, i, ī, u, ū, e, o, k, kh, g, gh, ṅ, c, ch, j, jh, ñ, ṭ, ṭh, ḍ, ḍh, ṇ, t, th, d, dh, n, p, ph, b, bh, m, y, r, l, ḷ, v, s, h, ṃ

A

*akataññū* — ungratefulness; (separate *akatu-ññu*) knowing the Uncreated.
*akālika* — timeless, intemporal.
*akuppa-cetovimutti* — unassailable deliverance of mind.
*acinteyya* — not to be speculated about, unthinkable.
*ajjhatta* — inside, internal, subjective (opp. *bahiddhā*).
*ajjhattakkāyā* — internal body.
*ajjhattikāyatana* — internal base.
*aṭṭha* — eight.
*atakkāvacara* — not in the sphere of reason or logic.
*attavāda* — belief in self.
*attā* — self.
*atthasaṃhita* — bringing advantage, profitable.
*saddhā* — faith, confidence.
*adhivacana* — designation.
*an-* — without (prefix).
*anattā* — not-self.
*anāgāmī* — non-returner.
*anicca* — impermanent.
*aniccatā* — impermanence.
*anupādisesa* — without residue.
*anuloma* — with the grain, in conformity (opp. *paṭiloma*).
*anulomikā khanti* — acquiescence in conformity.
*aparapaccayañāṇa* — knowledge not dependent or relying on others.
*appamāṇa* — measureless.
*abhikkanta* — gone forward, gone beyond.
*abhiñña* — direct knowledge, knowledge of supernormal success.
*arahat* — one who is worthy (usually untranslated).
*ariya* — noble (opp. *puthujjana*).
*ariyapuggala* — noble individual.
*ariyasāvaka* — noble disciple.
*avijjā* — nescience (opp. *vijjā*).
*asmimāna* — conceit '(I) am. ('Conceit', *māna*, is to be understood as a cross between 'concept' and 'pride' — almost the French 'orgueil' suitably

attenuated. *Asmi* is 'I am' without the pronoun, like the Latin 'sum'; but plain 'am' is too weak to render *asmi*, and *ahaṃ asmi* ('ergo sum') is too emphatic to be adequately rendered 'I am'.)
*anatimāni* — non arrogance.

Ā
*ākāsānañcāyatana* — the base of infinite space.
*ānāpānasati* — mindfulness of breathing.
*āneñja* — immobility, unshakability, imperturbability.
*āneñjasappāya* — suitable imperturbability.
*āneñjūpaga* — arrived at imperturbability.
*āyu* — life.
*āloka* — light.
*ārocita* — announced, called.
*āroceti* — to relate, to tell, announce, speak to.
*āvasati* — to live at or in, stay.
*āsava* — canker, intoxication.

I
*iddhi* — accomplishment; power (usually supernormal).
*indriya* — faculty.

U
*uddhacca-kukkucca* — distraction and worry.
*upakilesā* — imperfection, defilement.
*upadhi* — essential of existence.
*upādāna* — holding.
*upādiyi* — held.
*upādisesa* — residue.
*upāsikā* — female lay-follower.
*ubhato-bhāga-vimutta* — liberated in both ways.
*usmā* — heat.

E
*ekatta* — unity, identity, single state.
*ehipassika* [*ehi* + *passa* + *ika*] — of the Dhamma, that which invites every man to come to see for himself, open to all.

K
*kappa* — aeon, age.
*kamma* — action.
*kāma* — sensuality.
*kāmataṇha* — sensuality.
*kām'upādāna* — holding sensuality.
*kāya* — body.
*kāyika* — bodily.
*kuṭi* — cottage.

KH
*khandha* — aggregate, mass, totality.
*khīṇāsava* — destruction of the cankers.

C
*cakkhu* — eye.
*cakkhundriya* — eye-faculty.
*cakkhuppāda* — arising of the

eye (of knowledge).
*citta* — mind, consciousness, cognition, spirit, heart, purpose, (conscious) experience, &c. (*Citta* is sometimes synonymous with *mano*, and sometimes not; it is occasionally equivalent to *viññāṇa* in certain senses. Related to *cetanā*, but more general. Its precise meaning must be determined afresh in each new context.)
*cittakkhepa* — loss of mind, perplexity.
*cetanā* — intention, volition, will.

J
*jāti* — birth.
*jhāna* — meditation.

ṬH
*ṭhapanīya* — that (which) should be put aside.
*ṭhitassa aññathatta/ṃ* — invariance under transformation.
*ṭhiti* — station.

T
*takka* — reasoning, logic.
*taṇhā* — craving.
*taṇhakkhaya* — the destruction of holding.
*tayo* — three.

D
*dasasil-upāsikā* — ten precept laywoman.
*dāna* — gift, especially of a meal.
*dāyaka* — (male) giver.
*diṭṭhi* — view (usually, wrong view).
*diṭṭhigata* — going to, involved with, consisting of, (wrong) view.
*diṭṭhisampanna* — (one) attained to (right) view (= *sotāpanna*).
*dibbacakkhu* — divine eye.
*dukkha* — unpleasure (opp. *sukha*), pain, suffering.
*deva* (plural *devā*) — deity.
*dosa* — hate.
*dve* — two.
*dhamma* — thing, image, idea, essence, universal, teaching, Teaching, nature, natural law, ethic, ethical law, (cf. the Heraclitan 'logos').
*dhammacakkhu* — eye of the Dhamma.
*dhammapīti* — joy of Dhamma.
*dhammānusārī* — teaching-follower (opp. *saddhānusārī*).
*dhātu* — element.

N
*na* — not.
*nānatta* — difference, variety.
*nāma* — name.
*nāmarūpa* — name-&-matter.
*nibbāna* — extinction.
*nibbānadhātuya* — extinction element.
*nirodha* — ceasing, cessation.
*nekkhammasaṅkappa* — thought of renunciation.
*nevasaññānāsaññāyatana* — the

base of neither-perception-nor-non-perception.

P
*paccaya* — condition.
*pañcakkhandhā* — five aggregates.
*pañc'upādānakkhandhā* — five holding aggregates.
*paññā* — understanding.
*paññāvimutta* — deliverance by wisdom.
*paṭigha* — resistance.
*paṭiccasamuppāda* — dependent arising.
*paṭiloma* — against the grain (opp. *anuloma*).
*papañca* — dispersion, diversification.
*papañca-saññā-saṅkhā* — calculations of perceptions of diversifications.
*papañceti* — to diversify.
*parāmaṭṭha* — misapprehended.
*pariññā* — absolute knowledge.
*parinibbuta* — completely calmed, at rest.
*paritta* — limited.
*paripūrakārī* — fulfils. Or *paripūrī*.
*pasanna* — clear, bright.
*pāṭihāriya* — wonder, marvel.
*pātubhavati* — to appear.
*puññabhāgiyā* — having share in.
*puthujjana* — commoner (opp. *ariya*).
*punabbhavābhinibbatti* — coming into renewed being, re-birth.

PH
*phala* — fruit, fruition.
*phassa* — contact.

B
*bahiddhā* — outside, external, objective (opp. *ajjhatta*).
*bāhira* — outside.
*bāhirāyatānī* — external base.
*bodhipakkhiya* — on the side of awakening.
*bodhisatta* — creature pledged to enlightenment.

BH
*Bhagavā* — Auspicious One.
*bhaginī* — sister.
*bhante* — sir (monastic address, junior to senior; seniors address juniors, and equals to equals, as *āvuso*).
*bhava* — being, existence.
*bhavataṇhā* — craving for existence.
*bhāvetabba* — to be developed.
*bhikkhu* — monk, almsman.
*bhikkhunī* — nun, almswoman.

M
*magga* — path.
*manasikāra* — attention.
*mano* — mind (see *citta*).
*maṃsacakkhu* — fleshly eye.
*mahāthera* — great elder.
*mahābhūta* — great entity.
*mā* — don't; shouldn't.
*māna* — conceit.
*māyā* — illusion.

*micchādiṭṭhi* — wrong view (opp. *sammādiṭṭhi*).
*mūla* — root.
*mūlapariyāya* — root of all things.
*moha* — delusion.
*mohakkhaya* — destruction of delusion.

Y

*yoniso* — proper.
*yoniso* manasikāra — proper attention.

R

*rāga* — lust.
*rūpa* — matter, substance, (visible) form.

L

*liṅgā* — marks, characteristics.
*loka* — world.
*loka cintā* — thinking over the world, philosophy.

V

*vandanā* — worship.
*vijjā* — science, knowledge (opp. *avijjā*).
*vimokkhā* — liberation.
*vimutti* — deliverance.
*viññāna* — consciousness, knowing.
*viññānañcāyatana* — base of endless consciousness.
*vipāka* — ripening, result, consequence.
*vimokha* — liberation.
*vedanā* — feeling.
*vepulla* — full development, fullness.
*vematta* — difference, distiction.
*vohāra* — term, way of speech, common usage.

S

*sa-* — with (prefix).
*saupādisesa* — with residue.
*sa-upādisesa-nibbānadhātu* — extinction element with remainder.
*sakkāya* — person, somebody, personality.
*saṅkhata* — determined.
*saṅkhāra* — determination, determinant.
*sacca* — truth (plural *saccāni*).
*saññā* — perception, percept.
*saññāvedayitanirodha* — cessation of perception and feeling.
*satta* — seven
*saddhā* — faith, confidence, trust.
*saddhānusārī* — faith-follower (opp. *dhammānusārī*).
*saddhāvimutta* — released through faith.
*sappāya* — beneficial.
*samaṇabrāhmaṇa* — recluses and divines.
*samādhi* — concentration.
*samphassa* = *phassa*.
*sammādiṭṭhi* — right view (opp. *micchādiṭṭhi*).
*saḷāyatana* — six bases.
*sikkhā* — training.
*sīl* (Sn) = *sīla*.

*sīla* — virtue, (right) conduct.
*sīlabbata* — rites and rituals; conduct and customs.
*sekha* — one in training, (self-) trainer.
*sotāpatti* — attaining of the stream.
*sotāpanna* — stream-attainer.

H

*hita* — useful, suitable, friendly.

COLOPHON

Typeset at Path Press Publications
in Stempel Garamond SouthAsia (MacCampus)
using Adobe InDesign CS4 on Mac OS X
Printed on 100 grs. Munken Pure, FSC-certified
Bookproduction: Wilco, Amersfoort

PRINTED AND BOUND IN THE NETHERLANDS